Presented To:

_____

From:

_____

Date:

_____

Normal
Christianity

DESTINY IMAGE BOOKS BY JONATHAN WELTON

The School of the Seers

Normal Christianity

If Jesus Is Normal, What Is the Church?

Jonathan Welton

DESTINY IMAGE® PUBLISHERS, INC.

P.O. Box 310, Shippensburg, PA 17257-0310

"Promoting Inspired Lives."

This book and all other Destiny Image, Revival Press, MercyPlace, Fresh Bread, Destiny Image Fiction, and Treasure House books are available at Christian bookstores and distributors worldwide.

For a U.S. bookstore nearest you, call **1-800-722-6774.**

For more information on foreign distributors, call **717-532-3040.**

Reach us on the Internet: **www.destinyimage.com.**

ISBN 13 TP: 978-0-7684-3961-8

ISBN 13 HC: 978-0-7684-3962-5

ISBN 13 Ebook: 978-0-7684-8937-8

For Worldwide Distribution, Printed in the U.S.A.

1 2 3 4 5 6 / 14 13 12 11

Contents

FOREWORD

As a brand-new Jewish believer in Jesus, I got to know Kathryn Kuhlman. Miss Kuhlman had such an intimate relationship with the Holy Spirit that at every meeting, hundreds of major miracles erupted.

When she offered to mentor me, I made the biggest mistake of my life and said no. The reason I said no was because she was only doing what the Bible called "normal." As a new believer, I thought all believers walked in that same miracle power. After all, the only thing I knew was what I had read in the Bible. Take someone who has never read the New Testament and ask them to read it. Then tell them, "Miracles have ceased." They will not believe you.

I was convinced that what Miss Kuhlman did was normal. I was convinced that Jesus walked in miracles. I was convinced the apostles walked in miracles. I was convinced the disciples walked in the same miracle power. I was convinced the least disciple walked in the same miracle power of Jesus.

9

I quickly realized that only a few believers today walk in this same power. How did we lose the power that was available to the first church? Since God never changes, I will give you one guess as to who did the changing.

I want you to be normal! In other words, I want you to become a demonstrator of the miracles of the Kingdom of God. There has only been one biblical plan by God for evangelism. Because we have settled for dead religion, we have a cerebral Gospel. Few come to the Lord through logic.

Few Jewish people come to the Lord through apologetics. But I have led thousands of Jewish people to the Lord through signs and wonders. Once they see miracles, I have their undivided attention to proclaim the Gospel.

I believe before Jesus returns there will be two churches. One will be religious and the other will be *normal*. This book by Jonathan Welton will help restore your childlike faith, and you will become *normal!*

Sid Roth, Host
"It's Supernatural!" Television Program

CHAPTER ONE

WHAT IS NORMAL?

*What is the normal Christian life? We do well at the outset to
ponder this question. The object of these studies is to show that it is
something very different from the life of the average Christian.*
—Watchman Nee[1]

In 1886, Doctor John Pemberton, a pharmacist from Atlanta, Georgia,
created the first batch of Coca-Cola. Dr. Pemberton concocted the formula in a three-legged brass kettle in his backyard. The name was a sug-
gestion given by John Pemberton's bookkeeper, Frank Robinson. Being a
bookkeeper, Frank Robinson also had excellent penmanship, and it was he
who scripted "Coca-Cola" into the flowing letters of the famous company
logo. The soft drink was first sold to the public at the soda fountain in Jacob's
Pharmacy in Atlanta. Since its humble beginnings, Coca-Cola has become
world famous. Currently, more than 1.6 billion servings of Coca-Cola are
consumed every day in more than 200 countries. The company has been in
business for well over 100 years, employing nearly 100,000 people around
the world.[2]

This amazing rags-to-riches story begs the question, how does a product become such a market force that almost anywhere in the world you can find its influence? The short answer, *it tastes good.*

This is not a book about soda and its influence in the world. Having traveled extensively, I am conscious of the sad fact that there are many people familiar with Coca-Cola, even in deeply remote areas, who have never heard the name of Jesus.

How is it that the name of Jesus, which has had 2,000 years to spread, has not yet reached the whole world, whereas a soft drink can reach the world in 100 years? Even with approximately 500,000 churches in the United States of America, the Great Commission (see Matt. 28:19-20) has not yet been fulfilled. Why is this so? The short answer, *our Christianity doesn't taste good.*

In 1985, Coke decided to alter its secret formula. Coke had been slipping behind their competitor, Pepsi, and thought the answer would be found in a new blend. Coke's chief executive officer announced, "The best has been made even better!" But the announcement triggered a furor. Within days they were re-thinking their re-think. Coca-Cola reintroduced the old formula, calling it "Classic Coke." Within months, Classic Coke had overtaken Pepsi.[3]

When the original recipe, given by Jesus Himself, is altered, Christianity becomes undesirable. Fortunately, the Church is coming into a significant shift in the years ahead, restoring her to what I have termed "Normal Christianity." In this book, you will be re-presented with the original recipe that Jesus gave His Church. As a wise company once said, "You can't beat the real thing!"

REVIVAL

Christians from all walks of life often declare that what the Church really needs is a "revival." This is a statement that always brings a sly smile to my face. Please understand that there is no disdain in this look, merely the inquisitive entertainment that I enjoy from having heard hundreds of varied explanations of what the word *revival* means.

As I have traveled and ministered in many different denominations, I have heard countless definitions of *revival*. Gathering the many answers to "what is revival" has in some ways become a hobby of sorts. Over time, I have devised a way of understanding the opinions I have heard, placing them on a sliding scale.

My scale runs from 1-10, 1 being denominations considered conservative in doctrine and practice, typically the historic denominations (about 1.3 billion individuals worldwide).[4] When asked to define revival, an individual from this background will typically give a concise definition similar to this: *Revival is when God comes close to the Church and Christians repent of their hidden sins and non-Christians are convicted of their sins in the streets and cry out to God for salvation.* As one individual from this end of the scale stated to me, *"Revival is community awareness of God."* I summarize this viewpoint as God spontaneously coming close to the Church and people getting saved at an unusual rate. This is usually attributed to repentance of sin, which is somewhat confusing because then it is both the cause and effect of revival.

Now consider the perspective of the 10 on my scale. Here the denominations are of the Pentecostal or Charismatic type (about 707 million individuals worldwide).[5] When an individual from this end of the scale is asked to define *revival,* it is a much more complex phenomenon. First of all, the definition would be inclusive of everything on the scale from 1-9 and much more. This definition of *revival* includes the following: raising the dead, casting out demons, healing the sick, walking on water, multiplying food, power evangelism, angelic visitations, transport in the spirit between locations, as well as all nine of the Holy Spirit's gifts in operation. These experiences are major marks of what those on this scale of 10 define as *revival.*

In the past few years, I have noticed that Christians in this group have become so burned out on using the word *revival* that many of the leaders have started using new terms to communicate more specifically. Words such as: *cultural transformation, renewal, outpouring, reformation, restructuring, new wineskin,* and so on. Rather than throwing my personal definition on the pile, I have arrived at a conclusion. *I do not believe in revival!*

No matter where you are on the scale, most likely you are stunned by that statement, because every denomination believes in revival by some definition. I propose a totally different approach. Having looked at the Gospels and the Book of Acts, I would say that everything on the scale is expected of every Christian. It does not matter where you fit on the scale, God expects the Normal Christian to live as a 10 and more. In short, the New Testament does not present the idea of revival; it shows what a *Normal Christian* life looks like.

I know that this concept runs against the grain of many years of Protestant teaching. But as the late Walter Martin said, "Controversy for the sake of truth is a divine command."[6] We must break free from the wrong concepts that are holding us back.

Jesus and the Book of Acts are the standard of Normal Christianity. Remember the fad a few years ago when people wore bracelets reminding them, *"What Would Jesus Do?"* Christians state that Jesus is the example of how to live, yet this has been limited in many cases to how we view our moral character. When Christians tell me that they want to live like Jesus, I like to ask if they have multiplied food, healed the sick, walked on water, raised the dead, paid their taxes with fish money, or calmed storms. I typically receive bewildered looks, but that's what it is like to live like Jesus!

Perhaps we are ignoring a large portion of what living like Jesus really includes. While I agree that we are to live like Jesus, *"Those who say they live in God should live their lives as Jesus did"* (1 John 2:6 NLT). I am also aware that the application of Jesus' model has been minimized to something that can be accomplished by living a moral life. Many Christians believe that they can live like Jesus without ever operating in the supernatural. *Does that sound right to you after reading in the Bible about all of the miracles He performed?*

No Such Thing

If a group of Christians in a region began to seriously live like Jesus, in the full meaning of that reality, the rest of the Church would elevate them and claim that a sovereign move of God is taking place. When this happens, it creates an unfortunate separation that lessens the responsibility of the rest of the Church to also live like Jesus in fullness. When we see revival as a spontaneous phenomenon that happens randomly, we show our lack of understanding of the true nature of Christianity. We must begin to see that everything that has been defined as revival is considered normal by the Bible. As author Graham Cooke has said so well:

> Unlike inhabitation, there is no call for revival found anywhere in Scripture. The Church, quite simply, should never need reviving. Revival is not about getting people saved; revival is about the Church coming back to her original purpose before God. I think it's very sad that so many of us have prayed and longed for revival—it means the Church is a long way from what God wants us to be. Maybe, just maybe, a little touch from God could bring us immediately into line. That's the mystery of life with the Godhead—you just never know what could turn the tide of history.[7]

Consider the question, "How many revivals are in the Book of Acts?" This question is fundamentally flawed. My contention is that there is no such thing as revival in the New Testament; therefore, the answer is none. *Revival* is merely a word that has developed into many complicated interpretations. Yet the result has actually distanced the Church from what she is called to be. There are many interpretations that state, "The Church will be like Jesus when revival comes," which actually removes from our shoulders the burden of living like Jesus in the present.

Once more, everything that we have called revival, the New Testament teaches as Normal Christianity. I believe in Normal Christianity. Next I will explain the definition of two terms that will be used throughout this book: *Normal Christianity* and *Average Christianity.*

NORMAL AND AVERAGE

Average is a mathematical form of estimating. Let's say that Farmer John sells bushels of apples, and last week he sold 10 bushels. To find the average number of apples per bushel, you must add up the total number of apples, and then divide by the number of bushels, in this case, 10. This is how you arrive at an average of let's say 40 apples per bushel. Now if we were to take this a step further and say that Farmer Steve sold 15 bushels containing 50 apples each, this would mean that Farmer John is selling fewer apples on average than Farmer Steve.

Normal is a completely different system of measurement. Normal is based on comparing with an ideal. For example, a normal human being has 10 fingers and 10 toes. Notice that I am not saying that the *average* human being has 10 fingers and 10 toes, but a *normal* human being has these. That is because we are comparing all human beings against the concept of an ideal human being. The normal human being has two eyes, a nose, a mouth, and so forth. If a person were to be lacking in any of these areas, that person would not be considered below average, rather, that person would be abnormal. Abnormal means that there is an aberration from the standard of what is considered normal. Jesus Christ is the example of Normal for the Christian. To be different from Jesus in any way is to be an aberration from the standard set by His life.

Most Christians process their lives through averages, comparing their spirituality against the backdrop of neighbors, friends, their church family members, and relatives. When describing the type of church that they attend, typically comparisons are used for description. *"My church has great worship compared to the church I used to attend. My pastor gives boring sermons, not good ones like our youth pastor. We have a huge church, compared to the other ones in town."* The comparisons are endless. When describing revival, current spirituality (below average) is compared with what is described as revival (above average spirituality).

Consider how your mind automatically answers the following questions:

† Are you frequently angry?

† Do you have a lot of lustful thoughts each day?

† Do you swear often?

† Do you read your Bible enough?

† How strong is your prayer life?

The answers to these questions do not matter for my point to be made, but consider *how* you arrived at your answers. Most likely you arrived at your answers by comparison. Perhaps you compared with what you know of the people around you or the people who you look up to (or look down on). Maybe you even compared your current state to that of yourself in the past. Each of these ways of arriving at your answer reveals that you are thinking in the system of averages.

If you arrived at your answers by looking at Jesus as the example—He is the only measuring rod for your life—then you are one of very few people who think this way. This is the shift in thinking that we all must make: Jesus is the only measuring rod for what is considered Normal Christianity. If our lives do not resemble the life of Jesus, then the only definition for us is abnormal.

As long as we allow the wrong system of measurement, we will forever make the same error as the homeowner in the following Chinese proverb.

One day a man wanted to install a pipe on his oven. He measured the length with his ruler and asked the coppersmith to make a ten-foot long pipe. When the pipe

17

was delivered, it seemed to be a foot too long. It would not fit. He reprimanded the coppersmith for the mistake. The coppersmith measured it again with his own ruler and found it was exactly ten feet. But the customer insisted that it was a foot too long.

Finally, the coppersmith examined the customer's own ruler and discovered that it was sawed off a foot. The customer's child had done this as he was playing with this ruler. No wonder, then, that the measurement always ended up a foot longer.

Our systems of spiritual measurement are like this ruler, an untrustworthy standard. We must reorient all standards of measurement and look only at Jesus as the ideal. He is the only One against whom we should compare ourselves. He is Normal, and either we are Christlike, or we are abnormal. These are our only options. We must no longer get a false sense of comfort by comparing averages and perhaps finding that we are above average in our spirituality. Many above-average Christians are still abnormal. When we mistake average for normal, we end up far below what God established through Jesus as Normal.

Normal Is a Personal Responsibility

All revivalists, both past and present, have carried a high level of personal responsibility to live as Normal Christians, with Jesus as their role model. Revival is not something in outer space that must be drawn to earth through the right formula of actions. Revival does not even exist; it is merely a term for describing Christians actually living like Jesus. If we are going to shift out of the mindset of occasionally living like Jesus and call it revival, we must be willing to accept the fact that we are required to live as Normal Christians every day. This is our responsibility and is not contingent upon something sovereign that takes place outside of us. The question has never been, "Where is revival?" but the question should have always been, "Who is revival?" You and I are the answer to that question.

As a Normal Christian, I am revival (if we must use this term); revival is not something that occurs outside of me. Proverbs 26:20 says, *"Without wood, a fire goes out...."* Normal Christians pay close attention to the fire of their own spirits and are constantly gathering wood and feeding the flame of the Holy Spirit. Maintaining your own spirit and the fire of the Holy Spirit within you is how you sustain revival.

It is a major shift to understand that revival is a personal responsibility to live like Jesus. But it is the renewing of the mind that will lead to permanently sustained revival. Revival is not a matter of finding and implementing the correct formula. It is a matter of right perspective and lifestyle.

An Average Christian is like a *thermometer,* in that he or she can describe the spiritual climate to you. Normal Christians, however, are like *thermostats* because everywhere they go, they shift the atmosphere. Consider Jesus, the first Normal Christian, after the wedding at Cana (the beginning of His ministry). He was never again able to walk into any atmosphere and be a wallflower. Normal Christians affect change in every environment. This type of lifestyle is not accidental; it requires constant, personal responsibility.

I have found that one of the heaviest challenges to being normal is living in the present. Typically we want to worship at the altar of our past experiences, revivals, and the good ol' days, or we want to prophesy and declare about the future move of God. But the responsibility of living normal in the present is extremely unpopular. It is vital that we take up our personal responsibility every day, no matter the circumstances that surround us. The famous Normal Christian, Charles Finney, was once asked to define *revival.* He stated that revival is as simple as drawing a circle on the ground around yourself; within that circle, you have a revival.

NORMAL IS APPEALING

Many strategies have been implemented to make Christianity more appealing to the secular realm. Perhaps a funnier sermon, a new coat of paint, better music, a casually dressed pastor, and the list goes on—all in an attempt to re-present the Gospel in Above-Average packaging. What would happen if we were to throw out the standard ideas of Average thinking and try Normal thinking?

Think for a minute about the ministry of Jesus. He didn't have a building; He didn't have funny sermons, PowerPoint, music, and the like. Yet, Jesus had massive crowds. He was beloved of sinners, the government did not want to bother Him, and the only people who wanted to kill Him were the religious folks. The religious live comparing themselves with each other, and Jesus totally devastated their personal assessments because no Pharisee could ever measure up to Him. Jesus' life impossibly raised the average, and it made them all look bad. Shockingly, Jesus claimed to have set the *low bar* of what a Normal Christian is to be, *"I tell you the truth, anyone who has faith in Me will do what I have been doing. He will do even greater things than these, because I am going to the Father"* (John 14:12).

Average Christianity is rampant in the European and North American churches. Statistically, this is the most unattractive form of Christianity in the entire world. But back when Christians were normal, Simon the Sorcerer would have paid money to have what Peter had (see Acts 8). Sinners wanted to be with Jesus, but nowadays the world does not want to be with His followers. As Mahatma Ghandi put it so frankly, "I like your Christ. I do not like your Christians. Your Christians are so unlike your Christ."[8] We are called to be little-Christs, which is what the name Christian means. Normal Christianity is the most attractive thing in the entire universe. In the following quote, Watchman Nee describes the beauty of Normal Christianity.

From the Holy Scriptures we may see that the life as ordained by God for Christians is one full of joy and rest, one that is uninterrupted communion with God, and is in

20

perfect harmony with His will. It is a life that does not thirst and hunger after the world, that walks outside of sins, and that transcends all things. Indeed, it is a holy, powerful and victorious life, and one that constitutes knowing God's will and having continuous fellowship with Him.

The life which God has ordained for Christians is a life that is hid with Christ in God. Nothing can touch, affect or shake this life. As Christ is unshakable, so we are unshakable. As Christ transcends all things, we also transcend all things. As Christ is before God, so we are before Him. Let us never entertain the thought that we should be weak and defeated. There is no such thing as weakness and defeat; for "Christ is our life" as declared in Colossians 3:4. He transcends all; He cannot be touched by anything. Hallelujah! This is the life of Christ!

The life ordained for Christians is full of rest, full of joy, full of power, and full of the will of God. But let us inquire of ourselves as to what sort of life we are living today. If our life is not what God has ordained it to be, then we need to know victory. Hence, we shall look into this matter of our experience. And what we shall relate here may not be pleasing to our ears, because some of us are rather pathetic; yet we need to humble ourselves in order that we may see our lack and receive grace from God.[9]

What a beautiful description of Normal Christianity! I would like to build on Nee's thought by adding the supernatural element of the Normal Christian life as found in the New Testament. Every sentence in the next three paragraphs is paraphrased from Scripture. This is how the Bible describes Normal Christians:

Every normal Christian has a spiritual river of water flowing from their innermost being. This is the same river that flows from the throne of God and brings life and healing to the nations. This water quenched all their spiritual hunger. They now carry a fountain of water that releases eternal life everywhere that they go. They had each had an encounter and experience with the almighty God where they went through a mystical transformation of being born again. They were given the very mind of Christ. They walked as new creatures on this earth, as partakers of the divine nature. When they spoke, they considered their words to be the very oracles of God. They had prayer meetings where the whole building was shaken by the power of God. Their shadows falling on people caused healing to happen. Articles of their clothing were healing diseases, and they had so many ordinary miracles that they had to come up with a category of miracles called *extra-ordinary*. One of the Church leaders even rebuked them for acting like mere humans.

Their perspective was that they were seated in heavenly places, ambassadors sent from Heaven as representatives of God to bring reconciliation to all humankind. Everybody in the Church was considered a king and a priest, as well as a citizen of Heaven. The almighty Creator of the universe was known to them by other names, such as Friend, Beloved, and Daddy. When they performed miracles, sorcerers wanted that level of power so badly that they offered money for it. When they were persecuted and jailed, angels freed them from prison.

They had gatherings of people who were so hungry for God that they would meet all night—someone even died by falling out a window, and then they raised him from the dead. Then there was the time when a viper bit one of them on the hand and the poison didn't harm him at all; in fact, he held it over a fire until the snake fell off. They walked in so much spiritual power and authority that the Holy Spirit had to block them from going on one of their mission trips. This is what many of us would consider a revival of astronomical proportions, but I am convinced that according to the Bible, this is Normal Christianity.

ACTIVATION

At the end of each of the following chapters, there is an Activation section. The activation suggests an exercise that will help you put the truth of the chapter into practice. These are basic exercises intended to stretch your spiritual muscles and prepare you to walk as a Normal Christian. The truths in this book are deep and stretching. In order to get the most out of it, I strongly recommend that at the end of each chapter you stop, put in your bookmark, and complete the activation exercise. You will receive the best absorption of this material if you do. Most of all, enjoy and have fun growing!

ACKNOWLEDGMENT

Also at the end of the following chapters, I acknowledge people who have helped shape my spiritual life. I know it's not "normal" to intersperse these thank-yous throughout the book, but considering the focus of each chapter, it just seems right to do so.

I would like to personally thank Pastor Bill Johnson of Bethel Church in Redding, California. Your tireless work has taught a generation how to be truly Normal Christians. Your teaching has fed my spirit like none other, and I thank the Lord for you.

ENDNOTES

1. Watchman Nee, *The Normal Christian Life* (Fort Washington, PA: Christian Literature Crusade, 1975), 9.

2. http://www.thecoca-colacompany.com/ourcompany/index.html; accessed February 8, 2011.

3. "Coke dropping 'Classic' tagline from logo" *MSNBC*; http://www.msnbc.msn.com/id/28932986/ns/business-consumer_news; accessed March 23, 2011.

4. "Religions of the World"; http://www.religioustolerance.org/worldrel.htm; accessed March 10, 2011.

5. James Rutz, *Mega Shift, Igniting Spiritual Power* (Colorado Springs, CO: Empowerment Press, 2005), 25-27.

6. Walter R. Martin, quoted on *The Quotable Christian;* http://www.pietyhilldesign.com/gcq/quotepages/truth.html; accessed February 28, 2011.

7. Graham Cooke, *Drawing Close* (Grand Rapids, MI: Chosen Books, 2003),16.

8. Mohandas Gandhi, quoted on *Brainy Quote;* http://www.brainyquote.com/quotes/quotes/m/mohandasga107529.html; accessed February 9, 2011.

9. Watchman Nee, *The Life That Wins* (New York: Christian Fellowship Publishers, 1986), 1-2.

CHAPTER TWO

REVIVAL MYTHS

The problem exists between our ears. As a result, a transformation—a renewing of the mind—is needed. —Bill Johnson[1]

There exist in the Church myths that have kept Christians from living normally. These underlying beliefs permeate almost all branches of the Church. Even though as believers we all want revival, these thought patterns are counterproductive to actually receiving a move of God.

If we continue to subscribe to these ways of thinking, we can be assured that the moves of God will be hindered. The following five myths have sabotaged the moving of the Holy Spirit for many years.

MYTH #1: WE ARE WAITING OR PERFORMING FOR THE FULFILLMENT OF A PROPHETIC WORD.

Having traveled all across the United States, some of the most common things I hear about are the prophecies over each local region. No matter where I go, I inevitably end up talking to an excited individual who tells me of "prophet so and so" who prophesied that their local region or church would be the epicenter of the next great awakening in America.

Now obviously, not all of these can be true, because you can only have one epicenter; that is what qualifies it as the epicenter. But rather than debating the obvious flaw, I have a problem with the foundational issue that these prophecies raise.

Many of the people I speak to are waiting for those prophetic words to come to pass before they begin to live as Normal Christians. It is as if they say to themselves, *When God comes, I will....* But this shows a misunderstanding of the nature of our relationship with God. This type of thinking comes from a warped view of revival. Many define *revival* as a strong sense of God's presence and the Church impacting the world for Christ. Yet, that is not something that we should be waiting for; that is just Normal Christianity.

Are we waiting for a prophetic word to come to pass, and then God will finally come closer? Perhaps if we start an around-the-clock prayer center or fast or get enough Christians to unify in a region, then maybe we can twist God's arm and He will come down and visit us. Do you see the wrong perspective that exists? It is not about finding the magic formula before we start to live the way that God expects us to as Normal Christians. Although prayer, fasting, waiting on God, and unity are good things, they are often used as excuses for why a region is not experiencing revival.

"Draw near unto God and He will draw near to you" (James 4:8a NKJV). This verse throws a wrench in the gears of these wrong perspectives. God is not waiting with crossed arms to respond to our performance like an angry father. God wants to be close to His children whom He loves, but He will not force Himself upon us. He gave us the free will to choose how close to Him we want to be. The measurement of how close God comes is totally dependent upon us. We determine how much of His presence we really want.

How many prophetic words were needed in the New Testament to have a revival? Did the early Church gather dozens of prophecies over a region and then wait for a sovereign move of God to come? Or did the members just constantly abide in Jesus like He told them to in John 15? Not one prophetic word was waited for in the Book of Acts before they lived as Normal

26

Christians. Dear reader, sitting around waiting for an extra-biblical concept of revival to come is irresponsible.

MYTH #2: GOD WILL SOVEREIGNLY MOVE WHEN HE IS READY.

To walk as Normal Christians, we must shift away from some misconceptions regarding the sovereignty of God. Although God is sovereign, it is not His number one attribute. As Presbyterian pastor and author Dennis Kinlaw points out so well, God is first relational, not first sovereign:

> Many of my Reformed colleagues believe that God is a Sovereign who orders the affairs of our world by unilateral, irresistible decree. However, I believe this concept leads to a defective view of God, of man, of sin, and of salvation. I am convinced that sovereignty is a secondary category applied to God. Sovereignty could not have been a part of God's experience until the Creation, when he had subjects to rule.[2]

Our perspective of the Godhead leads to our understanding of sovereignty. The Hebraic perspective of the Godhead views the Father, Son, and Holy Spirit as equals seated around a table discussing the choices and decisions of eternity.

The Hebraic perspective seems accurate to what we see in Scripture. Consider the following, *"And God said, Let us make man in Our image, after Our likeness..."* (Gen. 1:26 KJV). Here we see God being relational and discussing the decision of creation within the Trinity. I imagine the Father, Son, and Holy Spirit sitting around a kitchen table in Heaven before the creation and dreaming up humankind together: smiling, laughing, imagining, and enjoying all the fun and love that will be enjoyed with these lovely human creatures. The Godhead is much more relational than many have understood.

It is a necessary shift for the modern Christian to see God as primarily relational and His sovereignty as no more than His secondary attribute. The heroes of the faith have interacted with God on the basis of relationship before sovereignty. Remember in Genesis 18 when God was preparing to destroy Sodom and Gomorrah the Lord said, "How can I do this thing without first telling My friend Abraham?" Then when God shared with Abraham, Abraham was audacious enough to bargain with God over the number of righteous. Also recall in Numbers 14 that God was going to destroy the Israelites, but relented when Moses debated with Him. Last, in Amos 3:7 we find that God does nothing without first telling His servants, the prophets. Normal Christians are aware that God is extremely relational.

Smith Wigglesworth was known to say, "If God is not moving, I will move Him." A statement like that may sound presumptuous or arrogant to those who have overemphasized the sovereignty of God. But seen correctly, Smith Wigglesworth was referring to the fact that the depth of his relationship with God would cause Him to respond and act because Smith had moved His heart.

The revivalist Charles Finney was strongly opposed in his day for what seemed to be his disregard for the sovereignty of God. At that time, many believed that revival was a sovereign move of God. Finney, however, taught that revival had more to do with turning the heart back toward God. Not that God simply came closer to the Church at a random time of His choosing, but that God came closer when the Church turned back toward Him. This disagreement was a point of sharp contention, but Finney's fruit speaks for itself.

In a six-month span of time, from September 1830 until March 1831, Finney preached in Rochester, New York, several nights a week and three times on Sundays. During this time, nearly the whole region was converted. Some estimates are as high as 90 percent of the population, and roughly 100,000 people in the area, including up to a hundred miles away, came to the Lord. It has also been recorded that as many as 85 percent of Charles Finney's converts remained Christians years later.[3]

Seeing God as relational and responsive is a major key to living as a Normal Christian. This is the difference between waiting for a sovereign distant God to finally fulfill His prophetic words, versus a relational God who comes upon hearts that are turned toward Him. Many people have focused not upon God, but upon their lack of His presence. What we focus on we increase, so if we focus on our lack of His presence, we will not be receiving more, but if we focus on God Himself, His presence will increase in our lives. If we draw near to Him, He will draw near to us (see James 4:8). We are not waiting for a sovereign move of God. We can be Normal right now!

Myth #3: Jesus performed miracles because He is God.

If Jesus only performed miracles because He was God, then how can I live like Him without becoming God myself? Many Average Christians answer this question by saying that Jesus performed miracles because He was God. Normal Christians, however, understand that He was setting an example for all Christians to follow. If we believe that Jesus performed miracles only because He was God, then how can we follow verses like, *"Those who say they live in God should live their lives as Jesus did"* (1 John 2:6 NLT).

Jesus became like us and limited Himself to human restrictions. By doing that, Jesus made His lifestyle completely accessible to us. Actually, Jesus didn't only expect us to do the same miracles, He expected us to exceed His record.

> *I tell you the truth, anyone who has faith in me will do what I have been doing. He will do even greater things than these, because I am going to the Father* (John 14:12).

The truth is, Jesus did not perform His miracles as God. He performed them as a perfectly sinless Man anointed by the Holy Spirit. Jesus completely emptied Himself of His divine powers when He became a man. Yet

His nature was still divine, or as theologians say it, Jesus was fully God and fully man.

Jesus said of Himself:

> *...Most assuredly, I say to you,* **the Son can do nothing of Himself,** *but what He sees the Father do; for whatever He does, the Son also does in like manner* (John 5:19 NKJV).

Therefore, Jesus did not perform miracles out of His divine nature. He became limited to human restrictions to show us how to live correctly. In Philippians 2, the apostle Paul laid a beautiful groundwork for understanding this dual nature of Jesus.

> *Your attitude should be the same as that of Christ Jesus: Who,* **being in very nature God,** *did not consider equality with God something to be grasped, but* **made Himself nothing, taking the very nature of a servant, being made in human likeness.** *And being found in appearance as a man, he humbled himself and became obedient to death—even death on a cross* (Philippians 2:5-8).

Jesus *made Himself nothing.* The Greek word used here for *nothing* means emptied. Jesus literally emptied Himself of His God powers to become a man. He was still God, but His miracles were an example for us to repeat, not for us to gawk at and declare that only God could do that.

Many times Average Christians say that they cannot live the same way Jesus did. Often their reasoning sounds like the following statement, "*Well, of course Jesus did that, He is Jesus! But I'm not Jesus.*" The belief that Jesus only did miracles because He was God leads to a lot of disempowered thinking. It separates the believer from God's expectation that we live like Jesus and removes our responsibility of being Normal Christians. Jesus lived the life that we are all called to live. The life He lived is truly the definition of Normal Christianity.

MYTH #4: WE ARE NOT IN THE RIGHT SEASON FOR GOD TO MOVE.

One of the biggest misconceptions is that revival comes and goes—it is not constant. The Word says that we are to move from glory to glory, which means always moving steadily forward (see 2 Cor. 3:18). But blended into the teaching of revival, the Church seems to advance to mountain tops and then decline into valley lows. Although the Bible does teach that there are such times in life that can be referred to as valley seasons, wilderness seasons, desert seasons, and so forth, this does not contradict the fact that every believer is meant to live advancing from glory to greater glory without taking a step sideways or backward. How can both of these concepts be true at the same time?

The answer isn't that we don't go through tough seasons in life; it is a matter of *how* we go through these seasons. If we go through them correctly, they can be the catalyst that launches us into the next level of glory. Let us examine more closely one of the main passages about the valley season.

> *Blessed are those whose strength is in You, who have set their hearts on pilgrimage. As they pass through the Valley of Baca* [weeping], *they make it a place of springs; the autumn rains also cover it with pools. They go from strength to strength, till each appears before God in Zion* (Psalm 84:5-7).

All of us go through the valley seasons of weeping; the only difference is *how* each of us goes through them. Those who have "set their hearts on pilgrimage" are the ones who, as they go through the valley of weeping, transform their valley into a place of springs and pools. We are assigned valley seasons so that we can transform the valley and actually go from "strength to strength."

God sent you through the valley so that you would take over the valley, not so that you would submit to the valley experience and live in depression for ten years.

There is no excuse for not progressing forward. There is no neutral and no retreat in Normal Christianity. Many Average Christians have tried to use the valley season as an excuse for not moving forward. Some have even thought that Jesus was so beat up by His wilderness experience that He needed angels to strengthen Him. Some might rationalize saying, "If Jesus needed angels to strengthen Him, then surely I will get chewed up by life too, at times."

Let's take a closer look at Jesus and His wilderness experience.

Then Jesus was led up by the Spirit into the wilderness to be tempted by the devil. And when He had fasted forty days and forty nights, afterward He was hungry. Now when the tempter came to Him, he said, "If You are the Son of God, command that these stones become bread." But He answered and said, "It is written, 'Man shall not live by bread alone, but by every word that proceeds from the mouth of God.'"

Then the devil took Him up into the holy city, set Him on the pinnacle of the temple, and said to Him, "If You are the Son of God, throw Yourself down. For it is written: 'He shall give His angels charge over you,' and, 'In their hands they shall bear you up, Lest you dash your foot against a stone.'" Jesus said to him, "It is written again, 'You shall not tempt the LORD your God.'"

Again, the devil took Him up on an exceedingly high mountain, and showed Him all the kingdoms of the world and their glory. And he said to Him, "All these things I will give You if You will fall down and worship me." Then Jesus said to him, "Away with you, Satan! For it is written, 'You shall worship the LORD your God, and Him only you shall serve.'" Then the devil left Him, and behold, angels came and ministered to Him (Matthew 4:1-11 NKJV).

We see in one Gospel that Jesus was led into the wilderness by the Spirit, and in another Gospel it says that He came out of the wilderness in the power of the Spirit (see Matt. 4:1; Luke 4:14). I believe that these carefully selected words show us that Jesus was so successful in defeating the devil's temptations that He received an upgrade.

Many people hold the view that Jesus was so beaten up by His fast and His encounter that He needed angels to come and tend to His wounds. Yet this perspective sticks out sorely in the ministry of Jesus. There would be nothing else that matches this assessment, and it only makes sense when seen through a personal lens of defeat. An objective view of this story reveals that Jesus handled the devil like a rag doll and totally defeated him. Then when all was complete, the angels came and "strengthened Him," not in the sense of restoring to Him what He had lost in battle, but taking Him from the level of strength He was operating in to a level of greater strength.

Did the angels bring Jesus a protein shake and pat His little head and say, "It's OK Jesus, that round is over." No, they brought a victorious Jesus a fresh, new, high-level anointing. They strengthened Him.

MYTH #5: WE CAN JUDGE WHAT
IS AND IS NOT A REVIVAL.

If a group of people began to live as Normal Christians, many would refer to this as an outpouring of revival. Eventually three groups of people would develop: those who join in, those who oppose, and those who stand by analyzing and asking questions.

Many times when revival breaks out, there are those who stand back and fold their arms asking, *"Is that really revival?"* This question is totally void of reason because since there is no such thing as revival in the Word, there is no test to judge by. When we observe what is labeled as revival, we are actually seeing an outbreak of Normal Christianity.

Another question that surfaces quickly is, *"How do we sustain this move of God?"* This question comes from a wrong perspective that regards revival as something that resides in outer space and shows up occasionally either for no particular reason or in response to implementing the right formula.

If we are to consider the question of sustainability, we must first recognize that our goal is to sustain ourselves as Normal Christians. Sustenance cannot be addressed apart from personal responsibility. As per Finney's statement, we must each maintain our own personal circle of spirituality in life. It is not the job of churches to spiritually feed the believer; it is a personal responsibility to feed oneself.

In conclusion, if the shift is made to disregard these myths, the believer will be capable of a much healthier walk with God. These myths have kept the Church from being normal for many years. It is time to shed the weights and move from abnormal to normal.

Activation

Consider which of the "revival myths" you have believed. Write yes or no next to each of the following to identify which ones have been a hindrance to you. On a separate sheet of paper, write two or three sentences describing the shift in thinking that you will make to move away from believing these myths.

1. Myth #1: We are waiting or performing for the fulfillment of a prophetic word.

2. Myth #2: God will sovereignly move when He is ready.

3. Myth #3: Jesus only performed miracles because He is God.

4. Myth #4: We are not in the right season for God to move.

5. Myth #5: We can judge what is and is not a revival.

Acknowledgments

Thank you to Heidi Baker, Leif Hetland, and Patricia King. You have shown the Church a *normal* lifestyle, which interacts with God through relationship. God is not your benevolent dictator; He is your Papa and your Lover. Thank you for your shining example to us all.

Endnotes

1. Bill Johnson, *When Heaven Invades Earth: A Practical Guide to a Life of Miracles* (Shippensburg, PA: Destiny Image, 2003), 27.

2. Dennis F. Kinlaw, *The Mind of Christ* (Nappanee, IN: Evangel Publishing House, 1998), 25-26.

3. Roberts Liardon, *God's Generals—The Revivalists* (New Kensington, PA: Whitaker House, 2008), 315-317.

CHAPTER THREE

LOVE, AFFECTION, AND THE FAMILY OF GOD

Power without love is reckless and abusive, and love without power is sentimental and anemic. —Martin Luther King Jr.[1]

Imagine with me a foggy morning in London, England, in the mid-1700s. The house is hustling and bustling with activity. As you awake, you overhear the other children, their excited chatter revealing that a sweet old gentleman is coming for a visit and that he might adopt one child from the orphanage today. This is wonderful news, as it has been quite some time since there had been any hope of adoption.

Like all the other children, you push and shove your way to the washbasin in hopes of washing soot and filth from your hands and face before the visitor arrives. Yet, in the background you begin to hear the headmaster's whistle blowing. It is time for lineup. Hurrying down the stairs and trying not to trip in your tattered, old leather shoes, you push your way into line. As you stand between seven children to your right and four to your left, you wonder once again, *Why would anyone adopt me rather than one of the other eleven?*

As you stand perfectly still, other questions and feelings wash over you like ocean waves. *Will anyone ever see value in me? Will I ever find a home where I will feel accepted? Might I one day be strong and free? Will anyone ever hug me and tell me that I am loved? Will I ever belong to a loving family?*

This story is played out in many of our spiritual lives every day. We have tried our best to act right so that we might feel accepted and loved in someone's eyes. We show our worth through our performance so that perhaps we will be valuable. Many have lived with thoughts like, *If only I prayed more, fasted more, read my Bible more, witnessed more, then I would feel the good pleasure of the Father's love upon me. I must not be **doing** enough for Him to **really** love me.*

We must move from this orphan thinking and realize that we are completely, radically, and unconditionally loved. It is time that we agree and say from the depths of our hearts, like the apostle John: *"How great is the love the Father has lavished on us, that we should be called children of God"* (1 John 3:1a). Our adoption is past, and we live *from* love, not *for* love.

LIVING FROM LOVE

"Teacher, which is the greatest commandment in the Law?" Jesus replied: "Love the Lord your God with all your heart and with all your soul and with all your mind.' This is the first and greatest commandment. And the second is like it: 'Love your neighbor as yourself.' All the Law and the Prophets hang on these two commandments" (Matthew 22:36-40).

The total summary of the Law and the Prophets comes down to loving in two directions, vertically and horizontally—vertically loving our Father in Heaven and horizontally loving our fellow humans. For hundreds of years, believers have struggled to walk in love. We strive and perform, but are constantly caught in the frustration of failure. We have been missing a major key to success in our love walk.

There is a prerequisite that we must meet before we can successfully walk in a lifestyle of love. We must first receive a constant flow of love from God. This is why the apostle John says, *"We love Him because He first loved us"* (1 John 4:19 NKJV). Before we can attempt to love God, we must make our first priority to receive love from Him. The reality is that we cannot even love God correctly until we are receiving His love.

Do you see it? God loved us first; this enables us to love Him back. We live our lives empowered from His love, not striving for His love. Many Christians have tried to love God out of their personal strength and striving. "I choose to love God, I choose, I choose." They declare their love all day long, but it never flows from their hearts. We must first understand that God loves us and learn to receive His love. If we do not start with this foundation, then we may waste years trying to get God to love us.

Orphan thinking stems from a misunderstanding of God's unconditional love. We already are His dearly beloved children. Jesus is the only Person who has ever perfectly demonstrated unconditional love; therefore, as Christians, we should have the best understanding of what unconditional love means. When the word *unconditional* is used, it is referring to how we as humans typically set parameters for our relationships, such as, "If you do this, then I will respond in this manner." Jesus, however, has broken the transactional nature of relationships by requiring nothing of us. His love is without conditions; He did not ask anything from us when we were lost in sin. As John 3:16 says, *"For God so loved the world that He sent His one and only Son, that whoever believes in Him shall not perish but have eternal life."*

God did not ask you to do anything before He would love you. Meditate on that for a moment. Without conditions, He chose to love you and act in love toward you. The apostle Paul reiterates this point in Romans 5:6-8:

> *You see, at just the right time, when we were still powerless, Christ died for the ungodly. Very rarely will anyone die for a righteous man, though for a good man someone might possibly*

dare to die. But God demonstrates His own love for us in this: While we were still sinners, Christ died for us.

The unconditional love of God is somewhat forceful and offensive to our way of thinking.

Jesus already died for you, before you were even born. So it does not matter what you ever do right or wrong, you will always be completely and unconditionally loved. The Lord says that He loves you with an everlasting love (see Jer. 31:3). You cannot mess this up. It is as if the Lord throws His hands up and says, "I do not care what you do or have done. I have already decided to absolutely love you no matter what, and you have no influence in changing that."

You are not able to make the Lord love you any more or any less. The born-again experience should come with a moment of revelation that God the Father totally loves you no matter what. You are not loved because of what you could ever do, but because of who you are; you are loved because you are His child, His son or daughter. The Christian life is merely choosing to receive His forgiveness and love. When Jesus died, He died for the sins of the whole world (see 1 John 2:2), and those who accept His love are adopted into His family. You may need to read this paragraph a few more times, because for many this requires a major shift in thinking. It may alter your lifestyle drastically.

Before we can love God and fulfill the first great commandment, we must first receive His unconditional love. Once we soak in the reality that we are unconditionally loved, our natural reaction is to love God back. The first great commandment is not something that we have to strive to fulfill, but is fulfilled by our natural response.

Even Jesus, who is our example for everything in life, had to first receive love from the Father, before He loved others. *"As the Father has loved Me, so have I loved you. Now remain in My love"* (John 15:9). And Jesus directs us to receive from Him and love others out of that love. This is how the flow of love works. Jesus received love from the Father; then He loved the disciples.

He directs His disciples to do the same thing, *"My command is this: Love each other as I have loved you"* (John 15:12). They were to align themselves under the flow of love from Jesus and, out of that, love each other.

If you do not get under the flow of the love of God, then what is the source of your love? Your personal strength, perhaps? If you try to love people out of your own strength, without having received from God as your Source of love, then you will always be limited to your own capacity of love. However, if God is the Source of love from whom you draw, then you can always pour out love to others because your Source of love is unlimited. Even if someone does not love you back, you can continue to operate in love because you receive your love from Father God. You can always flow in love at all times, because you are abiding in the love that is flowing into your heart from the throne of God. You have unlimited resources when you are abiding in Him.

Your Worth and Value

An important piece that the Church has been missing in *loving our neighbor* is that there is a prerequisite to be met. For us to *love our neighbors as ourselves*, we must first love our *self.* This has been a major struggle for many individuals.

The Church has placed great emphasis on how we are dirty, rotten sinners. This has blinded us to our inherent worth and value. The result is that every time we sin, we do not treat ourselves with the same unconditional love that God has for us. We beat ourselves up and become disappointed and angry at our failures. This is a sign that our love for ourselves is completely based upon our performance and is thus conditional.

I remember sitting on an airplane and hearing the Holy Spirit ask me this question, "If you gained one hundred pounds, would you love yourself the same?" I answered honestly that I would love myself less, and He said, "Then your love for yourself is conditional and performance based." I was shocked. I soon began to realize that we need to love ourselves with the same unconditional love that God loves with.

At this point, an important question to answer is, "How much worth and value do I really have?" Value and worth are always determined by what someone else is willing to pay for something. In our case, God was willing to pay for us with the death of Jesus (see John 3:16). Therefore, we are *of equal value to Jesus* in the eyes of the Father, or else He made a bad investment. This is a truth worth pondering.

To the degree that we love ourselves, we will be able to love those around us. If our love for ourselves is conditional, then our love for those around us will also be conditional. We must realize that we are totally and unconditionally loved; then we must begin to love ourselves in this same way. Only then will we be able to love our neighbors with the same unconditional love that we have for ourselves.

Jesus said that His followers were to be known by their love for one another (see John 13:35). This should be the outstanding characteristic of the Normal Christian. We must be known as the most loving group of people on the planet. We have been adopted as God's children and called to represent Him on the earth. We are meant to be releasers of the kindness of God, which leads people to repentance (see Rom. 2:4).

OUR REPUTATION

The Bible says we are to be known for our love. Unfortunately, Average Christians are typically known only for their political stances on issues such as abortion, gay rights, and corporal punishment. We have reputations that are not in line with what Jesus said. We are not known for our love. The world often has quite the opposite to say about us. As one Wiccan author has stated:

> The heart of the organized church is cold and without feeling....Wiccans come from every (Christian) denomination. While the doctrines of each believer's prior affiliation and upbringing are indeed deeply ingrained, the reason they have distanced themselves from their respective denomination is

usually due to the lack of love and spiritual warmth they feel in these organized forms of Christianity.[2]

The quote you have just read was taken from a book written by an author who is helping to integrate former Christians into a mixture of Wicca and Christianity. According to this author, the heart of the Church is "cold and without feeling." Rather than addressing this problem in the Church, many have strayed from the true faith into the comforts of false religions.

This raises the question, "Why don't Christians actually walk in expressive love like Jesus did?" I believe that one of the main reasons that Christians do not walk in love is because we are afraid of being hurt, rejected, or injured.

> *There is no fear in love. But perfect love drives out fear, because fear has to do with punishment. The one who fears is not made perfect in love* (1 John 4:18).

According to this verse in First John, love and fear are opposites; they are incapable of sharing the same time and space. They repel and displace each other. The danger of walking in love is that when we live in open-hearted relationships, we give others the opportunity to trample our hearts.

Many people who are living in fear will say that we must, *guard our hearts* (see Prov. 4:23a). But I believe that they are incorrectly using this verse to maintain their fears. This verse is used by those who fear in order to say that we must carefully watch how close we let people get to us emotionally. Yet Jesus lived with complete transparency and vulnerability. He never pulled away from anyone. Jesus never put up emotional guards or walls; instead He loved fully and freely.

Proverbs 4:23 actually means to watch over what is *in* your heart, not to keep people *away* from your heart. When you read the second half of the verse, "*...for it is the wellspring of life,*" notice how the verse is saying to watch what comes out of your heart, not who is coming into it.

We are to keep an eye on our motivations and the purity of our thoughts. God has never told us to keep people away from our hearts. In fact, the love that we are called to walk in *is not self seeking* (see 1 Cor. 13:5) and *always trusts* (see 1 Cor. 13:7). When we seek to protect ourselves and will not be vulnerable and transparent with our hearts and emotions, we are being selfish and lacking trust. If we really want to be like Christ, we must have a high value for vulnerability and transparency in our lives.

THE FORK IN THE ROAD

If you are going to walk in love, then you must choose not to walk in fear. Imagine yourself standing at a fork in the road. As you look at your map, you see that if you follow the road marked Love, it will take you into the Forest of Confidence where you will be surrounded with strong, healthy trees. Eventually you will arrive at the beautiful, open, green pasture of Freedom.

If you chose to journey down the other route, marked Fear, it will lead you through the briar patch of Insecurity, where every subtle movement you make touches you with a thorn prick of pain and fear. Ultimately, you will arrive at the penitentiary known only as Control. Love leads to confidence and freedom, whereas fear leads to insecurity and control. Whenever you see the fruit of control, you can tell that fear is at the root.

Control has been spreading throughout the Church because of a fear of failure. We must make a decision: Are we going to walk in love, which brings us into risky amounts of freedom, or are we going to live in fear of failure and try to control our flesh through rules and regulations? If we are going to be Normal Christians, we must return to freedom, and our freedom must spring from the deep root of love from God.

Many have tried to walk in freedom outside of God's law of love, but this produces an unhealthy counterfeit called *independence*. Freedom and independence are not the same. Freedom comes through self-control, whereas independence requires the control of the surrounding environment. Freedom comes because individuals are in control of their own lives and choices;

self-control enables a person to stay walking in love regardless of the circumstances. Independence is maintained by keeping others at a distance so they do not gain control over us. People who walk in independence do not walk in love. *The only way to walk in love is to walk in freedom.* All other forms of freedom are gained through rebellion or isolation. And when we isolate ourselves from others, we are stepping into the danger zone of selfishness (see Prov. 18:1).

The natural expression of fear is to create rules, whereas the natural expression of love is affection and freedom. What we fear, we try to prevent through control, and what we love is allowed freedom so that it has room to grow.

KEEPING UP APPEARANCES

If we are going to walk in expressive love and vulnerability, one way that this is powerfully expressed is through physical touch. Whether through a handshake, hug, or holy kiss—affection is a biblical tool for expressing love.

Yet, because Average Christianity has suffered from so many moral failures among its leadership, the common reaction is to create rules, regulations, and boundaries. Some pastors never hug anyone in their congregations because they would not want to give the wrong impression. This concept is often filed under the rule of, *"Abstain from all appearance of evil"* (1 Thess. 5:22 KJV). The thinking is, if the affection that a leader gives could possibly be misinterpreted, then it is best to not express love in this manner. But think through the possible double standards with me.

If an evangelist comes to visit your church and he tells stories of how he goes down into the slums and hugs prostitutes and drug addicts to show them the love of God, we would most likely sit attentively, listening and asking God to give us a love like that. But what if after the message, the evangelist says that he will be waiting at the back of the church to hug people as they leave so they will feel the love of God—most likely we would be freaked out by such an unusual expression of love. Leadership may even be offended, thinking that this is an inappropriate display of affection.

So what is the conclusion? We would rather that an evangelist hug a prostitute to express Jesus' love, than that same evangelist give a Christian woman a hug in church. Is anyone else confused by this?

The truth is that in the King James Version of First Thessalonians 5:22 *("Abstain from every appearance of evil")* is a terribly misunderstood verse. If I were to say, "You have a nice appearance," it could be equivalent to saying, "You have a nice form." In this context, the two words are used interchangeably. Unfortunately, when First Thessalonians 5:22 uses the word *appearance*, instead of *form*, the whole meaning of the verse is changed. It is this contextual error that has caused so much confusion throughout the Church.

When you read this same verse in almost any other Bible translation, you will find that it is not saying that we should live in fear of what others will *perceive* as evil, but that we should avoid actual evil. Even the New King James Version corrects this mistake in First Thessalonians 5:22:

Abstain from every form of evil (NKJV).

Avoid every kind of evil (NIV).

Stay away from every kind of evil (NLT).

Abstain from every kind of evil (ESV).

Abstain from every form of evil (NASB).

We are called to live above reproach (sin), but not above suspicion. We are not supposed to live in fear of what others might misunderstand. It is obvious from the life of Jesus that He never cared what misunderstandings others might have. He healed people on the Sabbath, He told His listeners that they had to eat His flesh and drink His blood (see John 6:53-56), and

He even made statements that made people think that He was suicidal at times (see John 8:22).

Jesus was constantly under suspicion; He was harassed for hanging out with prostitutes, thieves, winebibbers, and tax collectors, and He had women of questionable character crying on Him and kissing His feet. If we are going to be like Him, we cannot live with so much concern for the opinions of others.

Biblical Affection

C.S. Lewis said, "Affection is responsible for nine-tenths of whatever solid and durable happiness there is in our lives."[3]

Greet one another with a holy kiss (Romans 16:16a).

Greet one another with a holy kiss (1 Corinthians 16:20b).

Greet one another with a holy kiss (2 Corinthians 13:12a).

Greet all the brothers with a holy kiss (1 Thessalonians 5:26).

Greet one another with a kiss of love (1 Peter 5:14a).

In the Mediterranean region during the first century, the cultural norm for close friends and family was to greet each other with a kiss. Paul and Peter understood that the mystery of our faith is that we have been spiritually adopted into the family of God. Therefore, we should also express love to one another. If we had been saved into an informal institution of God, then perhaps Paul and Peter would have recommended that we withhold affection until we have known someone for a few years. Instead they approached Christianity as adoption by God into a family, and healthy families are affectionate with one another. To differentiate between the common greeting and a greeting within the family of God, they referred to this expression of love among the brethren as a *holy* kiss.

This became the common practice of the early Church. This type of affection makes more sense in a church culture that suffered under persecution. Consider the fact that every time one would say goodbye to their friends, it might have been for the last time. Keeping in mind the cultural context, affection became quite normal during the first four centuries of Christianity. Consider Saint Augustine's instructions to the early Church.

> ...when the Sacrifice is finished, we say the Lord's Prayer which you have received and recited. After this, the 'Peace be with you' is said, and the *Christians embrace one another with the holy kiss.* This is a sign of peace; as the lips indicate, let peace be made in your conscience, that is, *when your lips draw near to those of your brother, do not let your heart withdraw from his. Hence, these are great and powerful sacraments.*
>
> —Saint Augustine of Hippo (A.D. 354-430)[4]

Because not all Christians live in the Mediterranean region—and none now who lived in the first four centuries of Christianity—what is the practical application of the holy kiss in our modern Western culture? I believe that the cultural equivalent of a holy kiss is an affectionate embrace. In fact, the name of one of the minor prophets was Habakkuk, which translated means *hug* or *embrace.* Prophets were, and are, specifically commissioned to represent the nature of God. It is interesting to note that God is so in favor of giving hugs to one another that even one of his prophets was named "hug." Maybe we need some "hug" prophets in our cold, religious institutions.

If we understand that the modern equivalent to a holy kiss would be an affectionate embrace, then we should ask the big question, "What would Jesus do?"

Now one of the Pharisees invited Jesus to have dinner with him, so He went to the Pharisee's house and reclined at the table. When a woman who had lived a sinful life in that town learned that Jesus was eating at the Pharisee's house, she brought an alabaster jar of perfume, and as she stood behind Him at His feet weeping, she began to wet His feet with her tears. Then she wiped them with her hair, kissed them and poured perfume on them.

When the Pharisee who had invited Him saw this, he said to himself, "If this man were a prophet, He would know who is touching Him and what kind of woman she is—that she is a sinner." Jesus answered him, "Simon, I have something to tell you." "Tell me, Teacher," he said. "Two men owed money to a certain moneylender. One owed him five hundred denarii, and the other fifty. Neither of them had the money to pay him back, so he canceled the debts of both. Now which of them will love him more?" Simon replied, "I suppose the one who had the bigger debt canceled." "You have judged correctly," Jesus said.

*Then he turned toward the woman and said to Simon, "Do you see this woman? I came into your house. You did not give Me any water for My feet, but she wet My feet with her tears and wiped them with her hair. **You did not give Me a kiss, but this woman, from the time I entered, has not stopped kissing My feet.** You did not put oil on My head, but she has poured perfume on My feet. Therefore, I tell you, her many sins have been for-given—for she loved much. But he who has been forgiven little loves little* (Luke 7:36-47).

To put this story into modern terms, Jesus was offended that Simon the Pharisee did not greet Him with an affectionate embrace. Jesus was pleased that the sinful woman had the freedom and love in her heart to express her love for Him. But the religious leader was essentially rebuked for his coldhearted, nonexpressive love.

Personally, having grown up in a physically expressive family, I have been surprised by the cold, nonexpressive love in churches for years. I sometimes compared my natural family with my church family and was grieved trying to figure out why the church was so rigid and nonexpressive to one another—especially since the Word commands us over and over again to kiss each other, and even Jesus was upset when He did not get His kiss (see Ps. 2:12; Luke 7:36-47).

William Shakespeare said it well, "They do not love that do not show their love."[5] Now I am not advocating that we all try to implement kissing each other at church, especially since this is foreign to our time and culture. But I do believe that we need to contextualize what the Word is telling us so that we can return to the healthy affection of Normal Christianity.

I believe that a big piece of Normal Christianity is *sharing* hugs. Notice that I have italicized the word *sharing*. I'd like to explain something that my spiritual grandmother taught me. Some people only *receive* hugs, and it is like hugging a tree trunk as they stand there awkwardly waiting for you to stop. Others *give* hugs; they are constantly hanging on and hugging everything and everyone. The healthiest scenario is when two people give and receive a hug at the same time; this is what Grandma called *sharing* a hug. The family of God desperately needs to *share* more hugs.

Anthropological and medical science has confirmed that Grandma was right! Considering the facts found through studying and promoting the positive effects of expressed physical affection, I would say that Grandma was ahead of her time.

In the Floyd [2003] study, undergraduate research assistants were distributed pairs of questionnaires with instructions to recruit one of the most affectionate people they knew and one of the least affectionate people they knew to take part in the study. The questionnaires in each pair were identical except that their identification numbers indicated that one questionnaire was to be given to the affectionate person and the other was given to be given to the non-affectionate person. Participants were told nothing about why they were being selected to take part; rather, the research assistants simply asked them to complete the questionnaire to help the assistants with a class project. Participants mailed their completed questionnaires directly to the researcher.

The questionnaires contained a battery of measures assessing individual and social-level variables. Floyd predicted that the high and low affection groups would not only differ from each other but also that the affectionate communicators would be advantaged relative to the non-affectionate communicators. At the individual level, he hypothesized that highly affectionate people would be happier, have higher self-esteem, be less stressed and less depressed, and have better overall mental health than would the less affectionate people. He also proposed that they would be more comfortable with interpersonal closeness and less fearful of intimacy. At the social level, Floyd predicted that highly affectionate people would be more socially outgoing, would receive more affectionate communication from others, would be more likely to be in a romantic relationship, and among those who were in romantic relationships, would be more satisfied with those relationships than would less affectionate people. The sample consisted of 109 individuals who ranged in age from 10-60 years.

Despite the relatively small sample size, comparisons between the high and low affection groups confirmed each of these predictions. Specifically, compared to low affection communicators, high affection communicators were happier, more self assured, more comfortable with interpersonal closeness, less fearful of intimacy, less likely to view relationships as being unimportant, less stressed, less likely to be depressed, in better mental health, more likely to engage in regular social activity, more likely to be in an ongoing romantic relationship, and (among those in a romantic relationship) more satisfied with their relationships.[6]

And in another study:

Some research suggests that the benefits of receiving touch are not just physical, but intellectual as well. Steward and Lupfer [1987] reported that college students who were touched lightly on the arm by their instructors during a one-on-one conference scored more than half a standard deviation higher on a subsequent examination (in either introductory psychology, American history, or government courses) than did students who were not touched by their instructors during the same type of conference (see also Foa, Megonigal, & Greipp, 1976).[7]

I have conducted my own social experiment of sorts. A few years ago I led a youth Bible study in a local (secular) café near my home. There were about 30 youth on a typical Thursday night. Each week we would gather and worship together by playing CDs. We had several traditions that made our group unique. One tradition was called, "The Hugging Song." Actually, this was just a song that we had designated as "the hugging song." The idea was that when we heard the initial drum roll at the beginning of the song, everyone knew that this was the hugging song and that we had approximately three and a half minutes to hug every person in the café. Instantly, we had 30 teenagers climbing over tables and chairs to hug every person—including customers who had walked in off the street to get a cup of coffee.

What a different culture this group had created. The non-Christians were surprised and would often stay through the entire Bible study, because they actually felt love from a group of Christians—what a novel idea! There were regular attendees who had come from broken homes, and this was the one time during the week when they were hugged and felt like they were loved and part of a family. Not everyone, however, was comfortable with this aspect of Kingdom culture. People who were bound by legalism, living in fear, or coming from a broken place in their hearts had the hardest time with the hugging song.

A BIG SHIFT

My long time friend, Mark Young II, shared with me how being part of the coffee house group caused a personal transformation to occur in his heart.

I was raised in an affectionate family. I fondly remember when my father would come home from work and it would be what we had titled "tickle time." My father would chase my brother and me around the house, and we would run not really wanting to get away. He would eventually catch us, gently pin us to the ground, and tickle us until we could barely breathe. This is one of my fondest memories with my father.

That being said, I still firmly had the idea that affection was to be kept in the family, and I loved my family deeply and strongly. When I was only 11, Aunt Laurie and her daughters, my two younger cousins, moved in with my family. Within the past year, my aunt had lost her husband, and was diagnosed with advanced HIV, which had already become AIDS.

I became very close to her and my cousins in that time. A year later she passed away, mere weeks before Christmas. This was the beginning of me closing my heart. I remember that I had not seen my father cry about this situation. (I'm sure he did, my father is a good man, but I don't remember it.) I remember sitting on the bumper of my parents' car in our church's parking lot and making a vow that I never wanted to hurt like this again.

Less than a month later, even more deaths in my family occurred. My uncle, My grandma Peg, my great aunt, and a close family friend all passed away. I spent half of December and most of January attending funerals. I officially stopped caring and loving at that point, and for a 12-year-old boy that is a very bad thing.

Fast forward to 1999. I am now 16 and coming to a Bible study, because I do love the Lord. Loving God was safe, He was perfect, and not exactly visible. If God didn't show you affection it didn't matter, because He didn't show anyone affection. It's important to know that these were not my thoughts at the time. They are just how I now know I was feeling and reacting to life.

Suddenly, the most horrific thing I could imagine happened. The drum roll to Sonicflood's "I want to know you" played and everyone began to rapidly run around the cramped coffee house hugging each other. My anxiety level rose, I was not feeling comfortable, so I ran. I made a mad dash to the restroom, a single-person-use restroom, and I safely locked myself away. I would wait out the three minute song hidden in the room. To my dismay, people did not get the message and instead week after week I became "the target" everyone was aiming to hug.

Most people eventually just let me go. I slowly became more comfortable and hugged my close friends, the ones I had known for years, but beyond that I would head to the restroom and wait for everyone else to get done. One girl, Erin, always waited for the end of the song and would meet me as I came out of my hiding spot and greet me with a hug. I didn't know it at the time, and I don't think she did either, but God was using her to break something down in me.

My friend Jonathan Welton asked me one week why I didn't like to hug. I responded, "It's a personal thing, and it shouldn't be taken so lightly. You should only hug those you really care about." He nodded, "Yeah, but shouldn't you be able to hug your family?"

I had never really considered those people family. I mean I had heard it preached numerous times. "We are the family of God!" But no one really applies that in such a literal way... do they?

I can remember the moment it all changed. I was in the Friday night youth group, worship was amazing, and it was time for this to be my fixing moment. God then showed me how I was afraid to love and how I instead hurt people to protect myself. He showed me specific situations with my brother over the years. I knew that this had to be acted on. I went to my brother and apologized for all the times I had hurt him instead of loving him and we wept, on our knees, together. It was a true healing restoring moment for me.

From that time on, I became much more affectionate. Hugs have become something natural to me now; they are ways I can measure the depth of a relationship. Most people who know me now would never be able to imagine that I was once afraid of a simple hug.

The Family Paradigm

The only way that we can safely reimplement affection in the Church is if we receive a revelation of the family of God. When we can begin to walk together in the family paradigm, affection will be safe again.

> *Do not rebuke an older man harshly, but exhort him as if he were your father. Treat younger men as brothers, older women as mothers, and younger women as sisters, with absolute purity* (1 Timothy 5:1-2).

If we can begin to view our relationships inside the Church through the lens of a healthy, natural family, a culture of purity will be formed. In a natural, healthy family, it is never acceptable to sexually violate your sister or mother. The same is true in the Kingdom. According to Paul, all women are either "my sister or my mother," and incest is unacceptable in the family of God (the obvious exception is that when you marry your spiritual sister, she becomes your wife and the paradigm shifts).

When the mind is renewed to perceiving all Christians as siblings in the family of God, then sexual immorality will cease being the major problem it has been. However, the danger of compromise looms when unhealthy hearts and perspectives remain in individuals. The bottom line is that we are each called to walk in absolute purity, and a shift in perspective will help us toward that direction.

Because the modern Church has existed more as an organization and not as a family, we tend to view each other as simply men and women and not as siblings. Yet, when we put something into the wrong category, we treat it wrongly. When we do not understand the purpose of a thing, abuse is inevitable.

For example, take the way that a Westerner sees a pig. It is just an animal, and it can be eaten for breakfast. But to a devout Hebrew or Muslim, a pig is an unclean animal that should not be eaten. Because they categorize a pig, not as simply an animal, but more specifically, as an *unclean* animal, they avoid defiling themselves. It is time that the men of the Church returned to the biblical categories that it started with. Viewing all females to whom they are not married as either their sister or mother will encourage appropriate interaction between the genders.

This actually gives us more freedom, because in a family environment, I am not constantly afraid of being misinterpreted when I treat family members with affection. I am not under review by others for what my motivation might be. When we are walking as family, we are safe to express love. We can say, I love you, I value you, you are important to me. It is safe to hug one another or put an arm around each other. This is how a healthy family interacts.

The apostle John had a revelation of this kind of expressive love. Multiple times in the Book of John (which he wrote), He calls himself, "The one whom Jesus loved" and writes about his affectionate relationship with Jesus. *"Now there was leaning on Jesus' bosom one of His disciples, whom Jesus loved"* (John 13:23 KJV).

Normal Christianity measures spiritual maturity by love, not by theological knowledge. We need to become comfortable with expressive love because, if we are not comfortable with love, then we are not comfortable with God, because God is love (see 1 John 4:8).

For those of us who want to renew our minds to thinking like a Normal Christian, the family mindset is foundational. To those who are still operating in Average Christianity, this concept is quite foreign. Throughout the New Testament, we see the apostle Paul fathering individuals and constantly encouraging affection between the family that would be called his sons and daughters in the faith. The family dynamic is interwoven all through the New Testament, yet because of the many fears intertwined with Average Christianity, very few have taught from this perspective.

Activation 1

Imagine the love of God flowing down upon and over you like a waterfall. Just tilt your head back and receive this love for several minutes; ignore your surroundings and totally take in His love.

Activation 2

Think of your closest friends and family, and picture the women as your sisters and the men as your brothers. Examine how you would treat them differently if they were your actual blood relatives (if you have unhealthy blood relative connections, then view it through what an ideal family would be like). Begin to take the steps needed to walk in alignment with these pure thoughts.

Activation 3

I challenge you to stretch your "affection comfort zone" by being more expressive. Place three pennies in your left pocket today. Each time you stretch your comfort zone, move a penny from the left pocket to your right pocket. The goal is to move all three pennies every day. This is very subjective because each of us has a different comfort zone, so only move a penny if you feel that you have stretched yourself. Use your feelings as the system of measurement.

Acknowledgment

To the one person I have decided to learn to love for the rest of my life, to the one person I want to have a family with, to the one whose love has impacted me like none other—my wife, Karen Hannah. I love you, I love you, I love you.

ENDNOTES

1. Martin Luther King Jr., quoted on *GoodReads*, http://www. goodreads.com/quotes/show/134364; accessed February 28, 2011.

2. Nancy Chandler Pittman, *Christian Wicca; The Trinitarian Tradition* (Fairfield, CA: 1st Books Publishing, 2003), 1,8.

3. C.S. Lewis, quoted on *Brainy Quote*, http://brainyquote.com/ quotes/quotes/c/cslewis141013.html; accessed February 10, 2011.

4. Augustine, Sermon 227, *The Fathers of the Church*, (1959), Roy Joseph Deferrari, Genera editor, *Sermons on the Liturgical Seasons*, vol. 38, 197. See also Sermon 227 in *The Works of Saint Augustine: A New Translation for the 21st Century* (1993), Vol. 6, part, 3, 255.

5. William Shakespeare, quoted on *ThinkExist*, http://thinkexist. com/quotation/they_do_not_love_that_do_not_show_their_love-the/146736.html; accessed February 10, 2011.

6. Kory Floyd, *Communicating Affection, Interpersonal Behavior and Social Context* (New York: Cambridge University Press, 2006), 92-93.

7. *Ibid.*, 89-90.

CHAPTER FOUR

A SLAVE OF FREEDOM

The only way to deal with an unfree world is to become so absolutely free that your very existence is an act of rebellion. —Albert Camus[1]

Imagine a plantation owner in the southern United States in the early 1800s who declares to one of his slaves, "I set you free completely." This would be a wonderful gesture, but also an overwhelming revelation, one which the slave would have no ability to understand or live out. Given that the slave was captured in Africa and put into forced labor in another culture, on another continent, there would be no understanding of how to live as a free man in that society. The former slave would have to learn how to read and write, get a job, pay bills, feed his family, find housing, as well as traverse a whole host of new social situations.

As Christians, we are ourselves former slaves to the powers of sin and death. Then Jesus came and set us completely free. *"It is for freedom that Christ has set us free"* (Gal. 5:1a). When freedom was established in our lives at salvation, we were at first excited and overjoyed, but with time, many of us have struggled to walk in this new freedom. The revelation of moving from being *slaves to sin* into being *free in Christ* has been such a massive shift that we desperately need help being recultured.

In the plantation scenario, wouldn't it be great if the former slave had an individual who would teach him how to walk as a free man? I propose that this is exactly the job of Church leadership, to teach former slaves how to walk as spiritually free people.

Spiritual fathers have been entrusted by God to train sons and daughters how to walk safely in freedom. To oppose this, the devil has strategically planted fear in the hearts of many leaders to keep them from raising up other former slaves into free people. As long as a leader fears the failure of his children, he will be tempted to "protect" them from the dangers of freedom through legalism and control.

As spiritual fathers and mothers, we must learn to train others in freedom. If our children fail, we will continue to unconditionally love them, and God's grace through us will pick them back up. Love that motivates freedom is the difference between controlling leaders and empowering leaders.

Unbelievably Free

Let us pick up a train of thought that I began in the previous chapter. If all control comes from the root of fear, then what of having rules, standards, or boundaries in the Christian life? The first thing needed in order to grasp this topic is an understanding that we were created to live in total freedom. *"Then you will know the truth, and the truth will set you free"* (John 8:32).

Unfortunately, many people have tried to wield truth as a weapon. They try to force others to live in a certain way so that they do not violate so-called "truth." This type of *truth* becomes a burden to bear rather than something that brings joy and freedom. And at some point, we need to ask an obvious question, "What is truth, really?" (See John 18:38a.) Jesus said that He is *the Truth* (see John 14:6), so if Jesus is the Truth, then truth is not a concept to be obtained and observed, but actually a person to be embraced. When we embrace Jesus, we are embracing Truth, because Truth is a Person.

Unintentionally, many Christians have taken on a performance complex that subtly says, *the more I know Jesus, the more perfect I should be.* Yet, Truth and Jesus are one and the same; therefore, Truth always sets us free. If we follow this to its proper conclusion, we realize that *the more we know Jesus, the freer we become!* Yet, those who have lived in church the longest seem to be the ones with the most internal bondage. They have been trudging along under the weight of rules and regulations in hopes of walking in so-called truth.

Truth is a person to be known intimately. As you know Jesus, who is Truth, He sets you more and more free. If the truth that you are trying to bear up under is not bringing you into greater freedom, then it is not the authentic Truth of Jesus.

Jesus is not the only one trying to fill our lives with freedom. The Holy Spirit is also trying to bring us into freedom, *"Now the Lord is the Spirit, and where the Spirit of the Lord is, there is freedom"* (2 Cor. 3:17). Since the Holy Spirit dwells in the heart of every believer, the heart of the Christian should be the freest place on earth. The more we have the presence of the Holy Spirit in our lives, the freer we become. The more that we understand the unconditional love we have been given, the more confident we become in standing in our freedom.

At this point you may be wondering, *How much freedom does God really give me?* According to the apostle Paul, God has given you what I call ridiculous, scary, intense, overwhelming, and astounding amounts of freedom. Take a look at the following two statements from Paul:

> *"Everything is permissible for me"—but not everything is beneficial. "Everything is permissible for me"—but I will not be mastered by anything* (1 Corinthians 6:12).

> *"Everything is permissible"—but not everything is beneficial. "Everything is permissible"—but not everything is constructive* (1 Corinthians 10:23).

If I really believe what Paul is saying, then I am free to do everything, but I should choose not to do certain things because they will be neither *beneficial nor constructive,* and I should not be *mastered* by anything. This is the level of freedom that we are called to walk in. Unfortunately, many times the Church creates rules based out of culture and tradition, which encumber God's people from having total freedom. For example: You cannot dye your hair wild colors, you cannot drink alcohol, you cannot get facial piercings, you cannot listen to rock music, you cannot wear jeans with holes in to church, and so on.

But where do these rules fit with *everything is permissible?* In fact, none of these rules even have a biblical basis, and most of them were probably created out of the mistranslation of First Thessalonians 5:22, mentioned in the previous chapter. We have limited our freedom because we are afraid of how we may look to someone else. We were never meant to live in bondage; we were meant to walk in total freedom. In fact, Jesus describes the Normal Christian as being as free as the wind.

> *The wind blows wherever it pleases. You hear its sound, but you cannot tell where it comes from or where it is going. So it is with everyone born of the Spirit* (John 3:8).

The apostle Peter declared that we are to live as free men and women. *"Live as free men, but do not use your freedom as a cover-up for evil; live as servants of God"* (1 Peter 2:16). Our freedom should not bring us into a life of sin; if it does, then it is not from the Lord. Freedom comes from knowing Jesus (the Truth) and from the Holy Spirit. Where the Spirit is, there is freedom.

If the freedom that you are walking in leads you *into* sin, rather than *away* from it, you are getting your freedom from a source other than Jesus and the Holy Spirit. The closer you walk with Jesus, the more freedom you will walk in and simultaneously the less sin you will walk in.

As mentioned in the previous chapter, there is a difference between freedom and independence. Many times these two are confused and people end up fighting for what they believe to be freedom, only to end up with independence. Independent people actually give freedom a bad reputation. This counterfeit freedom lacks the deep heartfelt relationships that walking in freedom allows. Those who have experienced independence understand that it is a false, pretentious, and shallow version of freedom. To be independent requires keeping people away so they do not control you.

Independence allows people to do as they please, but ultimately it does not satisfy. Jesus best described what real freedom looks like in John 8:36: *"So if the Son sets you free, you will be free indeed."* Freedom that comes from walking in the love of God will never lead you into sin, but it will always lead you deeper into love and relationships. True freedom gives you the right to control yourself and make choices to walk in love.

Many Christian leaders are afraid to have their people walk in freedom because they do not know what choices their people will make. But if we teach people that their number one priority is to receive the love of God and walk in love toward others, then they will safely handle the freedom they are given.

Legalism

If you have grown up in the secular world, you may have struggled with sins such as drugs, fornication, drunkenness, or any other temptations that entangle people in the world. But if you have grown up in the Church, you typically encounter a different set of struggles. Having personally grown up in the Church, one of the biggest struggles that I have seen people deal with is legalism.

Legalism creeps in subtly and slowly. It starts when you look at people in the world and tell yourself that you do not want to be like *them*. And so, you find a way to surround yourself with rules and regulations, some sort of structure like a fortress to keep out all the evil stuff. The temptation to build a fence around yourself is very subtle.

I recently read an article in which the writer claimed that there is no such thing as legalism, because the word *legalism* does not occur in the Bible. The truth is that legalism is just a modern term for labeling a problem that has been around since the early Church. In the writings of the apostle Paul, he addresses the issue of legalism by another name, *tradition*.

The Pharisees counted 613 Laws in the Torah, consisting of 248 commands to action and 365 prohibitions. To make sure they did not break even one of these Laws by accident or ignorance, they created a hedge around the Laws. These hedges are called "Traditions" in the New Testament. The idea was to establish enough traditions around the Law that an individual would have to break a tradition before he could go all the way to breaking an explicit provision of the Law. Perhaps the best known example of these traditions is the thirty-nine acts prohibited on the Sabbath. For example, one of the laws of the Old Testament is not to work on the Sabbath (see Exod. 20:8-11). However, the religious leaders created a rule that a person cannot walk more than 4,854 steps at one time on the Sabbath because they did not want to break the rule about working on the Sabbath. This was called a, "Sabbath day's walk" (see Acts 1:12). This is an example of the kind of legalism that was added to God's laws. The Lord never said how far you could or could not walk on the Sabbath; in fact the Sabbath was actually created as a blessing to us, but with legalism like this, the Sabbath had been turned into a burden. That is exactly what legalism does; it creates burdens that God never intended.

The Average Christian lives under tremendous burdens of legalism. For example, why can I not dye my hair purple? Or have a Mohawk hair style? Or why not have a facial piercing? There is nothing in the Bible that addresses any of these, but the subtle idea that permeates the Church is that good Christians do not do these things. This is not in the Bible, and God did not give us these extra rules. We have created these rules based on our culture and tradition.

Both of my parents graduated from a Pentecostal Bible college, and they had grown accustomed to heavy legalism. Yet, as they grew over the course of 35 years of parenting, they observed that the more legalism that is applied (especially to children), the more the sin nature rises up. By the time I reached my high school years, my parents had switched their parenting methods to allow a lot more freedom. Please understand that my parents are very quiet, polite people, and I was very outgoing, extroverted, and somewhat radical as a young person. I am sure that at times it would have been easy to switch back to legalism and put barriers around me, but they stood firm in allowing me freedom.

As I watched many of my friends struggle under the weight of legalistic parents, I saw many of them go into rebellion to try to gain freedom for themselves. If only they had been given the freedom that God had intended, then they would not have had any reason to rebel. In fact, if all of the law can be boiled down to loving God and loving your neighbor as yourself, then any rule beyond that is unnecessary. Walking in love is the only law needed. As Paul says, "...*love is the fulfillment of the law*" (Rom. 13:10).

Average Christianity creates laws around laws and crushes people spiritually, and then it labels anyone who desires the freedom that God intended as rebellious. But God actually put that desire for freedom within us. God loves freedom so much that even after He gave freewill to the angels and they sinned, He still chose to give humankind freewill in the Garden of Eden. Freedom comes from the unconditional love that God has for us, whereas legalism comes from fear and control.

Let me share with you what freedom has looked like in my life. At this present time, I keep my head shaved clean all the time because I developed male pattern baldness in my early 20s. At times when I have guests over to the house, they are amazed to see my wedding photos where I have a full head of hair, and they wonder if that is really me in those pictures. But for my friends who knew me in my high school years, they know, as Paul Harvey would say, *the rest of the story.*

Not only did I used to have hair, but I had dyed my hair every possible color imaginable: purple, green, blue, yellow, orange, red, pink, white, silver, black. There were times when my friends' parents would ask my parents why they allowed me to do such a thing. The answer my parents gave changed my life. "We have our son's heart, so why does it matter what color his hair is?" If only more parents would focus on having the hearts of their children and stop focusing on the outward appearance, we would have much healthier families.

Likewise, our churches would be healthier if they were not so focused on outward appearances (as the Lord said to Samuel) and looked instead as the Lord sees, on the inward heart (see 1 Sam. 16:7). Focusing on the heart would result in less rebellion in the Church and in Christian homes. It is important that we do not fall into the same trap as the Pharisees:

> *Woe to you, teachers of the law and Pharisees, you hypocrites! You clean the outside of the cup and dish, but inside they are full of greed and self-indulgence* (Matthew 23:25).

Consider the following questions before you read on.

1. What rules do I have in my personal life?

2. Where did they come from?

3. What am I afraid of? From what are these rules intended to protect me?

4. Would I be willing to change these rules if the Holy Spirit directed me to do so?

God Is Not a Slave Owner

There are times when I get stuck on a verse for weeks and sometimes even months. Galatians 5:1 is one of those verses. *"It is for freedom that Christ has set us free."* Have you ever thought, *Why did Jesus die for me?* This verse gives an astounding answer: He wanted us to be free. Really? Doesn't that seem a little oversimplified to you? Yet this is what the Bible tells us.

As I considered the overwhelming reality of this verse, I realized that many Christians have lived as if Jesus performed a prison transfer. The mentality is, *I used to be a slave of sin, now I am a slave of Jesus. I moved from one prison to another.* But Jesus did not perform a prison transfer; He said that He came to *"...proclaim liberty to the captives..."* (Luke 4:18 NKJV). The Christian life is not summed up in the idea that I used to be satan's slave and now I am Jesus' slave. Yet this is how many Christians live and perceive what Jesus did.

Even Jesus disapproves of this idea:

> *I no longer call you servants, because a servant does not know his master's business. Instead, I have called you friends, for everything that I learned from My Father I have made known to you* (John 15:15).

The truth is that we are not His slaves, but we choose to be His bondservants. According to the Old Testament Law, a bondservant was given freedom and then made a choice to give his life to his master.

> *Now these are the judgments which you shall set before them: If you buy a Hebrew servant, he shall serve six years; and in the seventh he shall go out free and pay nothing. If he comes in by himself, he shall go out by himself; if he comes in married, then his wife shall go out with him. If his master has given him a wife, and she has borne him sons or daughters, the wife and her children shall be her master's, and he shall go out by himself. **But if the servant plainly says, "I love my master, my wife, and my children; I will not go out free,"** then his master shall bring him to the judges. He shall also bring him to the door, or to the doorpost, and his master shall pierce his ear with an awl; and he shall serve him forever* (Exodus 21:1-6 NKJV).

Jesus made us completely free of sin, satan, and death; and we chose to become His bondservants. This was the understanding of the early Church fathers.

Paul, a bondservant of Jesus Christ... (Romans 1:1).

Paul and Timothy, bondservants of Jesus Christ... (Philippians 1:1).

James, a bondservant of God and of the Lord Jesus Christ... (James 1:1).

Simon Peter, a bondservant and apostle of Jesus Christ... (2 Peter 1:1).

Jude, a bondservant of Jesus Christ... (Jude 1:1).

There is a large difference between a slave and a bondservant. Bondservants have worked off all their debts. They have no obligation to stay and be slaves any longer, but they choose to stay because of love for their master. This is the biblical perspective of a Normal Christian. We *choose* to serve our Lord because of the love we have for Him.

When you were a captive, the image of God in you had come under enslavement to sin. Jesus came to change that because He loves you, and it is an awful thing for the image of God to be enslaved to sin. Jesus' mission is summarized in saying that He set you free just so that you would be free. This freedom Jesus gave you is so important to maintain that Paul goes on to say, *"Stand firm then and do not let yourselves be burdened again by a yoke of slavery"* (Gal. 5:1). Now that you have been set free, stay free. For a Normal Christian, most spiritual warfare is not about getting out of sin, but maintaining freedom from sin or legalism.

In the Church, we must stand firm against the traditions of people. Legalistic traditions were trying to creep into the early Church, and the apostle

Paul, a former Pharisee himself, spent much time warning the Church not to allow this insidious evil into the Church. Paul wrote very harshly against legalism. *"This matter arose because some false brothers had infiltrated our ranks to spy on the freedom we have in Christ Jesus and to make us slaves"* (Gal. 2:4).

Essentially, those attacking the Church were saying, "The freedom that they have is so contagious that it is taking over the known world. If we are going to stop this move of God, we must use legalism and tradition to poison the spiritual atmosphere of freedom. That will trip them up. That will keep this movement from spreading."

> *"You foolish Galatians! Who has bewitched you? Before your very eyes Jesus Christ was clearly portrayed as crucified. I would like to learn from you just one thing from you: Did you receive the Spirit by observing the law, or by believing what you heard? Are you so foolish? After beginning in the Spirit, are you now trying to attain your goal by human effort? Have you suffered so much for nothing—if it really was for nothing? Does God give you his Spirit and work miracles among you because you observe the law, or because you believe what you heard?"* (Galatians 3:1-5)

It is for freedom that you have been set free. Let this concept sink deep into your heart; *God wants you free.* When God sent Jesus to pay the wages of your sin (see Rom. 6:23), He was not trying to buy a slave. God wanted free people who would choose to become His bondservants out of love for Him. God is not a slave owner.

THE LAW OF LOVE

To actually live a life free from sin, how many rules do we need in our lives? This is a subtle question that is asked in hundreds of different ways, thousands of times a week, all around the world. Jesus boiled down all of the 613 Old Testament rules and regulations into two rules, built on one foundation.

"Teacher, which is the greatest commandment in the Law?" Jesus replied: "'Love the Lord your God with all your heart and with all your soul and with all your mind.' This is the first and greatest commandment. And the second is like it: 'Love your neighbor as yourself.' All the Law and the Prophets hang on these two commandments" (Matthew 22:36-40).

Although we examined these verses in the previous chapter, I need to expand on a few thoughts and connect our freedom to the foundation of love. According to Paul, *the power of sin is the law* (see 1 Cor. 15:56). So every time we try to prevent sin by adding another law, we are actually digging ourselves deeper into a hole. There is no freedom in the bottom of that hole. No matter how far we dig down, all we will find is more dirt. Rules do not defeat our sin nature. In fact, Colossians 2 says that rules lack any power to restrain us from sin.

*Since you died with Christ to the basic principles of this world, why, as though you still belonged to it, **do you submit to its rules**: "Do not handle! Do not taste! Do not touch!"? These are all destined to perish with use, because they are **based on human commands and teachings. Such regulations indeed have an appearance of wisdom,** with their self-imposed worship, their false humility and their harsh treatment of the body, **but they lack any value in restraining sensual indulgence*** (Colossians 2:20-23).

The natural question that an Average Christian would ask is, *"What boundaries do you use to protect yourself against failure? Surely it is wisdom to have some rules, right?"* The answer to these two questions boils down to two basic options about how we can choose to live our lives.

OPTION #1: LIVE BY THE LOVE OF LAW.

We can live by a set of made-up rules. The problem is that our sin nature looks for a way around the rules we set. Apostle Paul said that the power of sin is the law (see 1 Cor. 15:56; Rom. 7:5). Therefore, sin is actually empowered when we set rules. For example, if the rule is "do not have sex with anyone other than your spouse," then your sin nature will look for a way around this rule. The sin nature is constantly on the lookout for loopholes around the rules.

In this case, the sin nature will operate in lustful thoughts rather than acting out and actually breaking the rule. This was the exact problem that Jesus addressed:

> *You have heard that it was said, "Do not commit adultery." But I tell you that anyone who looks at a woman lustfully has already committed adultery with her in his heart* (Matthew 5:27-28).

Jesus was speaking to the fact that the sin nature looks for loopholes around the law.

The sin nature may even look for a way around the rule by redefining the parameters of the rule, such as saying that certain sexual acts are not actually "sex." That way the claim can be made that the rule has not actually been violated. The sin nature is always on the lookout for a way around the rules. Rules do not stop us from sinning; the sin nature will always rise up correspondingly to find loopholes. As more rules are made, more fuel is put on the fire of our flesh.

OPTION #2: LIVE BY THE LAW OF LOVE.

The law of love is this: *I choose not to sin because it harms relationship.* Whenever we are walking in awareness of love and relationship, we naturally follow in the footsteps of Jesus. *"Jesus replied, if anyone loves Me, he will obey My teaching..."* (John 14:23a). It is not that we obey to prove that we love

73

Him (that has been the way the Church has misinterpreted what Jesus actually said), but that when I walk in love, my attention changes from focusing upon the rules to focusing on relationships. The apostle Paul explains the law of love so clearly in the following passage:

Let no debt remain outstanding, except the continuing debt to love one another, for he who loves his fellowman has fulfilled the law. The commandments, "Do not commit adultery," "Do not murder," "Do not steal," "Do not covet," and whatever other commandment there may be, are summed up in this one rule: "Love your neighbor as yourself." Love does no harm to its neighbor. Therefore love is the fulfillment of the law (Romans 13:8-10).

As the famous author Henry Lewis Drummond wrote in 1890:

If you love, you will unconsciously fulfill the whole law. You can readily see for yourselves how that must be so. Take any of the commandments. "Thou shalt have no other gods before me." If a man loves God, you will not need to tell him to put away other gods. Love is the fulfilling of that law. "Take not the Lord's name in vain." Would a man ever dream of taking the Lord's name in vain if he loved Him? "Remember the Sabbath day to keep it holy." Wouldn't a man be glad to have one day in seven to dedicate more exclusively to the object of his affection? Love would fulfill all these laws regarding God.

In the same way, if a man loves others, you would never think of telling him to honor his father and mother. He could not do anything else. It would be preposterous to tell him not to kill. He could not do anything else. You could only insult him if you suggested that he should not steal—how could he steal from those he loved? It would be superfluous to beg him not to bear false witness against his neighbor. If he loved him it would be the last thing he would do. And you would never dream of urging him not to covet what his neighbors had. He would rather they possessed it than himself. In this way "love is the fulfilling of the law." It is the rule for fulfilling all rules, the new commandment for keeping all the old commandments, Christ's one secret of the Christian life.[3]

The difficultly of developing this type of lifestyle is that we must have our eyes focused not on a list of rules, but upon walking in love in our relationships. Before I act, I am constantly aware of the pleasure or displeasure of the Holy Spirit and those around me. Every possible rule created outside of the law of love is a failing attempt at curbing the sin nature. The Average Christian has grown quite accustomed to living in awareness of a list of rules, rather than living in awareness of the heart of God. It will require a major shift for an individual to walk in true freedom.

I have shifted to only one rule in my personal life: *I choose not to sin because it harms relationship.* I have seen that those who live by the *law of love* rather than *love of law* actually end up obeying far better than those who are struggling to maintain the rules.

Consider the fact that with all our rules, guidelines, and legalism, we have not yet found a method for preventing sin within the Church. Many denominations are searching for the right formula or the right set of rules to keep people out of sin. So I would ask the question at this point, *"How is that working for you?"* Having all the rules just right does not give you power over temptation. Although scary, it is time to scrap what is not working and go back to love and freedom. You can safely walk in total freedom as long as you follow the law of love. Never do anything that violates love and the relationships in your life. Follow the law of love, and do not burden yourself with any of the *sin empowering rules* (see 1 Cor. 15:56).

To finish out these thoughts, we must address the issue of how we will respond when someone fails at walking in freedom. It is with this thought in mind that we must add to *love* and *freedom* a third concept, *grace*.

GRACE IS MORE POWERFUL THAN SIN

It is told that during a meeting on comparative religions in Britain, many scholars gathered together to discuss what, if anything, was unique to Christianity. Many different elements were discussed and debated. Was Christianity unique because of its concept of truth? No, other religions have this. Was it unique because of the doctrine of reconciliation? No, other religions have this. Was it unique in terms of inspiration of a particular book? No, again, other religions have this. It is told that C.S. Lewis entered the room during the debate and asked what the discussion was all about. "We are discussing what makes Christianity unique, if anything." "That is easy" Lewis responded, "It is grace."[4]

How does grace make Christianity different from any other religion in the world? Grace is what empowers our walk of love and complete freedom. If we are going to walk in the law of love, we will still make mistakes at times, but we always have grace propelling us to walk like Jesus. There is a constant flow of grace from the throne of God to us that empowers our walk of unconditional love. Consider the following verses from Romans, which tell us that to whatever degree we walk in sin, grace will always overpower:

> *Since we have now been justified by His blood, **how much more** shall we be saved from God's wrath through Him* (Romans 5:9).

> *For if, when we were God's enemies, we were reconciled to Him through the death of His Son, **how much more**, having been reconciled, shall we be saved through His life* (Romans 5:10).

*But the gift is not like the trespass. For if the many died by the trespass of the one man, **how much more** did God's grace and the gift that came by the grace of the one man, Jesus Christ, overflow to the many* (Romans 5:15).

*For if, by the trespass of the one man, death reigned through that one man, **how much more** will those who receive God's abundant provision of grace and of the gift of righteousness reign in life through the one man, Jesus Christ* (Romans 5:17).

*The law was added so that the trespass might increase. But where sin increased, **grace increased all the more*** (Romans 5:20).

The perspective of the Average Christian is, *If I sin too much, I may run out of grace.* But in the early Church, there was such a revelation of the overwhelming amount of grace available to us that Paul actually warned them to not continue sinning and thus abuse this abundance of grace. *"What shall we say, then? Shall we go on sinning so that grace may increase?"* (Rom. 6:1). This is exactly the opposite perspective of the Average Christian.

We have lived in fear that grace might possibly run out. Paul was essentially telling them, "You have an ever-abundant supply, much more grace that is always ever-flowing and overflowing, pouring and pouring and pouring and pouring. You have so much grace that it changes you into another person; you will not continue to walk in sin, and you will live dead to sin."

Grace actually changes the one who receives it. When you are walking in love and perhaps fail and violate the law of love, you need God's grace to empower you. When you receive this grace, it cleanses you, forgives you, and puts you back on track in your walk of love. His grace frees you from the fear of living without legalism. The fear of living without legalism is always, *What if I fail?* This fear leads to establishing rules all around you.

The truth is that you probably will fail, but why does that matter? You are unconditionally loved whether you walk in perfect love or whether you fail from time to time. You do not need to live in fear of failing, so long as you understand that you have grace to lift you when you fall.

When you make mistakes, there is grace. No matter what the mistake, no matter how big the mistake, if you seek repentance, there is grace for it from God and (one would hope) from the Church. Many have understood that God will forgive them for any failure, but the questions that remain are: Will His representatives give me grace? Will those who are supposed to reflect His image forgive me? Will those who are supposed to be little-Christs forgive me? Will they extend grace? Will they allow me freedom again when I fall, or will they then box me in as much as possible to try and fix me so I don't fall again?

> *Brothers, if someone is caught in a sin, you who are spiritual should restore him gently. But watch yourself, or you also may be tempted* (Galatians 6:1).

The Average Christian interprets Galatians 6:1 this way: "If someone is caught in a sin, put as many rules as you can around them to ensure that they never make that mistake again." If someone falls into sin, we try to restore them by placing them under a weight of legalism. Yet consider the nature of restoration. To restore something is to put it back in the place it was before the loss. The state of a Normal Christian is walking in love and total freedom. This should be the focus of all restoration.

The ideas that I have presented in the previous two chapters require major shifts in thinking. If you can picture in your mind that the legalism you have lived under for so long has put chains around your hands and feet in the spirit, it will help you process this shift. In a sense, coming into freedom can hurt, because you are taking off chains that have been there, in some cases, for decades. Perhaps the areas on your ankles and wrists where the chains have been will get sunburned for the first time in years and require ointment. But ultimately, freedom is worth it, and you should push forward toward making the full transition so that one day you can, as Paul said, *stand firm in your freedom.* And as Peter said, *live as free men and women.*

ACTIVATION

Consider the following questions again. This time write your answers to each with as much detail as possible. I believe that the Holy Spirit will speak to you regarding the increase of freedom He intends in your life.

1. What rules do I have in my personal life?

2. Where did they come from?

3. What am I afraid of? From what are these rules intended to protect me?

4. Would I be willing to change these rules if the Holy Spirit directed me to do so?

Now ask this additional question:

1. How might I trade my rule for the law of love?

DEDICATION

To the apostle Paul. Thank you for your tireless efforts to keep the Church free from legalism. You are my hero, and I look forward to meeting you one day.

ENDNOTES

1. Albert Camus, quoted on *ThinkExist,* http://thinkexist.com/ quotation/the_only_way_to_deal_with_an_unfree_world_is_ to/346776.html; accessed February 10, 2011.

2. Dr. Ron Moseley, *Yeshua: A Guide to the Real Jesus and the Original Church* (Clarksville, MD: Messianic Jewish Publishers, 1996), 90.

3. Henry Lewis Drummond, *The Greatest Thing in the World* (Springdale, PA: Whitaker House, 1981), 13-14.

4. C. Michael Patton, "My Grace Awakening: Thank You Chuck Swindoll," *Parchment and Pen Blog* (March 28, 2008); http://www.reclaimingthemind.org/blog/2008/03/my-grace-awakening-thank-you-chuck-swindoll/; accessed Febuary 10, 2011.

CHAPTER FIVE

THE CLEAN CONSCIENCE

*May we not deceive ourselves, imagining that sinning is inevitable
for a Christian, I think no thought hurts our Lord more than this.*
—Watchman Nee[1]

Imagine with me an old wooden ship named *The Conscience*. This ship is a powerful vessel of transport and can also wage incredible warfare. It has been proven through every fight and every storm. On the deck of this ship is a large, wooden cargo box with the word *Faith* stamped on it. *The Conscience* is only vulnerable in one way. If it crashes into a reef, the hull can be breached and the cargo will be lost overboard. Knowing this, the enemies of *The Conscience* have built reefs everywhere, because when *The Conscience* crashes, *Faith* is lost overboard. *"Holding on to **faith and a good conscience**. Some have rejected these and so have **shipwrecked** their faith"* (1 Tim. 1:19).

Throughout the New Testament, the words *faith* and *conscience* are often found together because they are intricately connected. This is why the apostle Paul gave Timothy a word-picture of how these two are connected.

Here is an example of what I think it looks like when sin defiles *The Conscience* and *Faith* sinks.

I step out of a wonderful time in the presence of the Lord and walk down the street. I happen upon a person in a wheelchair. Now, I know that sickness is not God's will because there are no sick people in Heaven, and Jesus said that things should be, *"On earth as it is heaven."* Therefore, I introduce myself and say, "I believe God wants to heal you. May I pray for you?" I pray for him, he gets healed, he accepts Jesus for salvation, he gets baptized in the Holy Spirit on the sidewalk, he gets delivered of the demonic influences in his life, and he joins a church. That is just another great day in the Normal Christian life.

Now repeat the exact same scenario, but change just one thing.

I step out of a wonderful time in the presence of the Lord and walk down the street. Suddenly, a lustful thought goes through my mind. Perhaps I entertain this thought for a moment and this sin defiles my conscience. Now my conscience is being convicted and my faith collapses. As I am walking along feeling condemned, I happen upon the person in the wheelchair, except this time my faith has already been crushed under the weight of a defiled conscience and there is no confidence to pray for healing in that moment.

Sin is the reef that breeches the hull of *The Conscience* and causes *Faith* to sink. When *The Conscience* is clean and healthy, we can sail through life with confidence.

This then is how we know that we belong to the Truth, and how we set our hearts at rest in His presence whenever our hearts condemn us. For God is greater than our hearts, and He knows everything. Dear friends, if our hearts do not condemn us, we have confidence before God (1 John 3:19-21).

The heart of the Normal Christian is maintained at rest in His presence. We need to understand how to quickly deal with a defiled conscience.

When you sin and are convicted, take these steps and you will recover your faith: 1) repent quickly, 2) receive cleansing for your conscience, and 3) get back up in full faith. The most obnoxious thing you can do to satan is quickly repent and step back into your identity. This is like a slap in the devil's face. He spent all that time carefully laying a trap for your feet, and you just repent and move on. Oh, how infuriating this must be for him!

Our Reputation

One day, while in a New Age shop doing outreach, I noticed a peculiar bumper sticker. It read, *"Water baptism: guilt and shame from the very first drop."* I struck up a conversation with the shop owner and asked him what the perspective of the bumper sticker was stating. He shared with me how there are many New Agers who have come from some type of Christian background. One of the main complaints from this group of people is that Christianity is filled with guilt, shame, condemnation, insecurity, hellfire, brimstone, and the like.

Unfortunately this is not an overstatement of the way Average Christianity has treated people. Many Christians continue to struggle year after year under a burden of self-imposed guilt and remorse for their sins and mistakes. Yes, the Holy Spirit does convict us of sin, but many have continued to beat themselves up for sins that have already been forgiven. The guilt and shame of our mistakes seems to stalk us long after we have been forgiven. Many of us never move from the initial experience of being a *sinner saved by grace* into the more mature life of being a *saint of the Most High*. What most in the Church need is a clear view of how God sees them and how they should be viewing themselves.

I find the story of Sarah to be a great insight into how God views us, both before and after repentance.

Then they said to him, "Where is Sarah your wife?" So he said, "Here, in the tent." And He said, "I will certainly return to you according to the time of life, and behold, Sarah your wife shall have a son." (Sarah was listening in the tent door which was behind him.) Now Abraham and Sarah were old, well advanced in age; and Sarah had passed the age of childbearing. Therefore Sarah laughed within herself, saying, "After I have grown old, shall I have pleasure, my lord being old also?" And the LORD said to Abraham, "Why did Sarah laugh, saying, 'Shall I surely bear a child, since I am old?' Is anything too hard for the LORD? At the appointed time I will return to you, according to the time of life, and Sarah shall have a son." But Sarah denied it, saying, "I did not laugh," for she was afraid. And He said, "No, but you did laugh!" (Genesis 18:9-15 NKJV).

This is the historic account of how Sarah responded in the natural. It is important to note that Sarah's laugh, according to the original Hebrew root words in this passage, was a mocking type of laugh. She was not saying, "Oh Lord, You are so funny." She was frustrated and angry toward God, scoffing at His declaration. This is not a response of great faith; it is as far in the opposite direction as she could get. Yet look at how God remembers this story in the New Testament.

By faith Sarah *herself also received strength to conceive seed, and she bore a child when she was past the age, because she judged Him faithful who had promised. Therefore from one man, and him as good as dead, were born as many as the stars of the sky in multitude—innumerable as the sand which is by the seashore* (Hebrews 11:11-12 NKJV).

Just those first three words alone are shocking. In Genesis, Sarah is laughing, mocking, and certainly not full of faith. And then later, she conceived a child, and God proved Himself faithful. Somewhere along the way she repented, and God rewrote her story. Fast-forward to the writing of Hebrews, and I can imagine God saying, "OK, this is how I want you to write this down. 'By faith Sarah...'" I wonder if the writer of Hebrews had a hard time writing this, yet this is how the Holy Spirit directed him to record her story. In the eyes of God, repentance literally rewrites your life story.

Like Sarah, when you repent, God changes your history and sets you back on the path of your destiny. If He did not do this, then the moment you made your first mistake you would be doomed—to never reach your destiny. Your sin would have permanently derailed you. Fortunately, *God interacts with you from your destiny, not your history.*

What Can Separate Us?

If we do not realize that God changes our history when we repent, we will continue to see ourselves through a reality that, according to God, no longer exists. If He changed our past, and we do not make the transition to seeing our past through His eyes, we are submitting ourselves to a false reality. God goes so far as to tell us that the past does not belong to us.

> *So then, no more boasting about men! All things are yours, whether Paul or Apollos or Cephas* [Peter] *or the world or life or death or the **present or the future**—all are yours, and you are of Christ, and Christ is of God* (1 Corinthians 3:21-23).

All things are yours, including the present and the future, but *the past* is not yours, and that is why He excluded it from the list. Your past does not belong to you; it belongs to God, which is why He can rewrite it as He so chooses. He goes on to say that your past can separate you from His love.

*For I am convinced that neither death nor life, neither angels nor demons, neither the **present nor the future**, nor any powers, neither height nor depth, nor anything else in all creation, will be able to separate us from the love of God that is in Christ Jesus our Lord* (Romans 8:38-39).

Most people read this verse and go on to conclude, *"Nothing can separate us from the love of God."* I would contend that *the past* was left off that list on purpose, because it *will* separate us from the love of God. God does not separate Himself from us, but when we access our past, we choose to turn away from Him. Because God does not exist in our repented-of past, we literally have to leave God behind when we delve into our past. We have to turn away from God to look into our past because God is in our future, and to look into the past we must turn our back on the future.

God does not want us to access our past apart from Him rewriting it. When we rehearse our past, we open the opportunity to repeat it. It is easy to fall into a cycle of repetition because our past (which repentance changed) does not lead us to our destiny. The repented-of past actually does not exist; therefore, to go back there is to live in a false reality. This false reality leads to a false present and a false future. The danger of rehearsing the past is the same thing that the ancient Israelites had to avoid.

*All these people were still living by faith when they died. They did not receive the things promised; they only saw them and welcomed them from a distance. And they admitted that they were aliens and strangers on earth. People who say such things show that they are looking for a country of their own. **If they had been thinking of the country they had left, they would have had opportunity to return. Instead, they were longing for a better country—a heavenly one.** Therefore God is not ashamed to be called their God, for He has prepared a city for them* (Hebrews 11:13-16).

If the Israelites had focused on the past, they would have found themselves repeating it. The problem is not the content of the past, but rather, our focus. We all tend to head toward where we focus, and as the old saying goes, *"If you don't change your direction, you will end up where you are headed."*

In Hebrews 11:16, it says *"God is not ashamed to be called their God."* This is not because they had a spotless past. God is not ashamed because they did not make the past their focus. It would have put God to shame if, after He had forgiven them, they choose to go back and rehearse the past over and over. That is a total disregard for God's forgiveness and shows no desire to move forward with Him. It is forgivable to make mistakes, and as long as they are put in the past, this does not shame God. But when we keep ourselves living in and from our past, we never move forward. God was not ashamed to be called their God, not because they had no past, but because the door was closed. The focus is not what is *behind* the door; the focus is *closing* the door.

Conviction Versus Condemnation

Many of us have been taught that we should remember our failures, because this is how we will learn from them. As revealed in this chapter, this is not how the Kingdom of God operates, and as such, it is not healthy for a Normal Christian. When we do not close the door to the past, the voice of *condemnation* begins to wreak havoc in our lives and destroy our confidence in Christ's forgiveness.

Webster's Dictionary says that condemnation is: "To declare to be reprehensible, wrong or evil, usually after weighing evidence and without reservation, to pronounce guilty, to deem unfit for use." Some synonyms are: to criticize, to sentence, or to doom.

Regarding those who have repented and received forgiveness by faith, the Bible says, *"Therefore, there is now **no condemnation** for those who are in Christ Jesus..."* (Rom. 8:1). God is not sitting in Heaven criticizing you, passing sentence on you, placing doom on you, or saying you are unfit for use, guilty without reservation, or reprehensible. God the Father never condemns His children. There is no condemnation in Christ.

Condemnation is a tool that satan tries to use against believers. If, after you repent, you continue to hear words in your heart declaring your guilt, you are hearing satan's voice of condemnation. At that point, it is best to command the voice of the demonic to be silent.

THREE TYPES OF CONVICTION

The Lord never uses condemnation to correct His children. He uses the much gentler voice of conviction. Conviction is defined as a convincing or being convinced. It is the job of the Holy Spirit to convince you when you have committed a sin. It is not His job to beat you and make you feel terrible.

Most of us know that the Holy Spirit convicts us of sin. However, most Christians do not realize that the Holy Spirit actually convicts us of three different things. *"...When He comes, He will **convict** the world of guilt* **[1]** *in regard to sin and* **[2]** *righteousness and* **[3]** *judgment"* (John 16:7-8).

1. Conviction of Sin

The Holy Spirit convinces our hearts that we have committed sin. We should then repent to God and/or to the person we hurt so that relationship can be restored. This is the first step of the three-step process of conviction that the Holy Spirit leads us through.

The Holy Spirit's voice is always going to come through love. God is love, and He always speaks the truth in love. We must reject the voice we hear in our hearts if it is saying, "I cannot believe that you are a Christian by the way that you have been acting. You sicken me, you are despicable, you are reprehensible, you should be ashamed." That is not a voice from Heaven, but one from the enemy.

2. Conviction of Righteousness

Once the Holy Spirit has convinced us of error and we have repented, He then begins to convince us of our righteousness. He says things like, "You are better than this; this is not who you are. I have read the end of your story. You are a mighty child of God, not a coward. You are the righteousness of God in Christ. Now, stand up tall, walk with confidence, walk in love, walk in strength. I have made you holy." This is the voice of the Holy Spirit convincing us of our righteousness in Christ Jesus.

3. Conviction of Judgment

Finally, the Holy Spirit convinces us to exact retribution upon the kingdom of darkness. This is not regarding judgment toward our sins. Our judgment was removed when we repented of our sin. In fact, John 16:11 explains that the conviction of judgment is in regard to satan, *"and in regard to judgment, because the prince of this world now stands condemned."* After we have repented and are convinced of our righteous standing with God, we are sent out to destroy the works of the enemy.

First, the Holy Spirit convicts people of their sin. After they repent, the Holy Spirit convicts them of their righteousness. The third step of conviction from the Holy Spirit reassigns them to go exact retribution from the tempting spirits that mislead them from the path of righteousness.

This is how God brings punishment upon satan. Once you are free from the very thing that kept you bound, perhaps even for years, whether lust, bitterness, shame, alcoholism, or something else, you are sent out to expose and crush these same works of darkness. The chains that bound you are given back to you for the whipping of the enemy.

Pre-Forgiven

Many have said that the Old Testament was *works-based salvation* and that the New Testament is *grace-based salvation*. The truth is that *faith* has always been the only way to righteousness in both the Old and New Testaments. *"For it is by grace you have been saved, through faith..."* (Eph. 2:8).

In the Old Testament, animal sacrifices were performed not as *works*, but in faith toward a coming Messiah. Sacrifices were but a proclamation looking forward to the day of Jesus' sacrifice (see Heb. 8:5; Col. 2:16-17). The Old Testament saints believed *forward toward* a coming Messiah whereas New Testament saints believe *back toward* the completed work of the Messiah. In both cases, it is a matter of faith, because people in both eras receive by faith from the same event in history—Jesus' death on the cross.

"He is the atoning sacrifice for our sins, and not only for ours but also for the sins of the whole world" (1 John 2:2). Jesus died not only for our sins but also for every sin ever committed. God already chose to forgive all sin for all time; now we must make the choice to receive His forgiveness by faith.

Like a steel cable suspended throughout all of eternity, Jesus' shed blood runs through the whole timeline. In A.D. 33, Jesus suspended a steel cable of forgiveness that stretches from eternity past to eternity future, it reaches infinitely in both directions. He established forgiveness for all sin and made it accessible by faith. Jesus' forgiveness was established before any humans were even created, Jesus was, *"...the Lamb that was slain from the creation of the world"* (Rev. 13:8). All that one must do is reach out and grasp it.

Imagine with me a man named Joe. In 1980, Joe accepted Jesus as his Savior. When Joe repented of his sins, Jesus had already forgiven Joe at the cross, but God's forgiveness was not applied to Joe until Joe received it by faith. In essence, Joe reached out into eternity and grasped the steel cable of forgiveness and pulled it into 1980. Jesus did not decide to forgive Joe in 1980. Jesus decided to forgive Joe in the year 33. It just took Joe coming to understand and grasp His forgiveness by faith.

Unfortunately, many Christians have thought that each time they sin, God must choose to forgive them again. Some have reached the point where they do not even want to ask forgiveness again because they have repented hundreds of times previously. This has led to the feeling that we have to convince God to forgive us once more, in hope that perhaps this time we will not sin again. We think God must be tired of choosing to forgive us again and again. Or the thought may be, *If I were God, I would have stopped forgiving me by now!*

The truth is that God made one choice to forgive all sin forever. Therefore, He never has to choose to forgive again. To put it another way, we have been *pre-forgiven* for anything we could do. When we sin, we are not coming to God to *ask* Him to forgive us; He already has! We are coming to God to *receive* His forgiveness by faith. *"And by that will, we have been made holy through the sacrifice of the body of Jesus Christ once for all"* (Heb. 10:10).

Even when God confronts us and convicts us of our sin, it is for our benefit. In human relationships, many confrontations are approached with a demand that the violator must apologize enough to earn forgiveness. However, when God comes to address us, He has already forgiven us, and He is coming not to demand an apology, but to show us our sin so that we stop. Repentance is not a matter of epic tears, but a change of direction. Change is brought about not from condemnation and guilt, but from a loving and forgiving Father. He comes to show us the destruction of our ways. It is *"...God's kindness* [that] *leads you toward repentance"* (Rom. 2:4).

You do not have to convince God to forgive you, because He already has. You need to accept the fact of His complete forgiveness, before, during, and after you sinned. If you sin, you do not need to convince God that you are worthy of a second chance. *You have been preemptively forgiven* for anything you could ever do. Jesus' death provided a perfect sacrifice so that all your sins could be covered once for all time (see 1 Pet. 3:18; Rom. 6:10; Heb. 7:27; 10:10). You must continue to receive your forgiveness by faith.

THE CONSCIENCE

Even though we have been forgiven, when we sin, we violate part of our human spirit called the conscience. The conscience is a spiritual organ within us that the Holy Spirit speaks to when He convicts us of sin. Our sin stains our conscience, and only blood can cleanse our conscience of this stain.

We must choose to draw near to God to receive cleansing from the guilty conscience.

Let us draw near to God with a sincere heart in full assurance of faith, having our hearts sprinkled to cleanse us from a guilty conscience and having our bodies washed with pure water (Hebrews 10:22).

In the Old Testament, the blood of the animal sacrifice did not have power to cleanse the conscience. Animal sacrifice done in faith, connected people to forgiveness, making them right with God, but it did nothing to cleanse the conscience of the individual who had sinned. Speaking of the Old Testament sacrificial system, it says in Hebrews:

This is an illustration for the present time, indicating that the gifts and sacrifices being offered were not able to clear the conscience of the worshiper (Hebrews 9:9).

The law is only a shadow of the good things that are coming—not the realities themselves. For this reason it can never, by the same sacrifices repeated endlessly year after year, make perfect those who draw near to worship. If it could, would they not have stopped being offered? For the worshipers would have been cleansed once for all, and would no longer have felt guilty for their sins. But those sacrifices are an annual reminder of sins, because it is impossible for the blood of bulls and goats to take away sins (Hebrews 10:1-4).

The blood of goats and bulls and the ashes of a heifer sprinkled on those who are ceremonially unclean sanctify them so that they are outwardly clean (Hebrews 9:13).

We see from these verses that in the Old Testament, the animal sacrifice only made a person outwardly clean. This left the conscience unappeased of the pain of sin and failure. As Hebrews 10:3 says, although the Old Testament people were forgiven, they still felt guilty for their sins. In the New Testament, Jesus placed His blood on the conscience so that we can be free from the guilt of our failures.

> *How much more, then, **will the blood of Christ, who through the eternal Spirit offered himself unblemished to God, cleanse our consciences from acts that lead to death**, so that we may serve the living God!"* (Hebrews 9:14)

Once Jesus shed His blood, we are not only forgiven, but now our consciences can be cleansed from the guilt and shame of failure. Jesus' blood provided forgiveness once for all sin. However, our conscience becomes defiled over and over again as we sin in life. His cleansing of our conscience was not once for all, but is in an ongoing process of being cleansed each time we stain it with sin.

The state of the conscience for the Normal Christian is clean from all guilt, sin, and conviction.

> *The goal of this command is love, which comes from a pure heart and a **good conscience** and a sincere faith* (1 Timothy 1:5).

> *I thank God, whom I serve, as my forefathers did, with a **clear conscience**, as night and day I constantly remember you in my prayers* (2 Timothy 1:3).

> *They* [Bishops] *must keep hold of the deep truths of the faith with a **clear conscience*** (1 Timothy 3:9).

Cleansing the conscience is not just a matter of seeking forgiveness because forgiveness is received by faith. Cleansing comes from applying the blood of Jesus to the conscience. For example, when you commit sin, approach the Lord this way: *1) God, I repent of _____ (insert sinful action), 2) by faith I receive Your forgiveness. 3) Lord, I have defiled my conscience, and I ask that You would sprinkle Your blood upon me for cleansing.*

According to Hebrews 10:22, when our conscience is defiled, it is cleansed by the sprinkling of His blood upon it. We receive His forgiveness by faith, but we must also by faith apply His blood to our hearts to cleanse our consciences.

PAINFUL MEMORIES

We now understand that God has forgiven us for all our sins—past, present, and future—and Jesus' blood can cleanse our defiled consciences. However, what about the sins that others have committed against us? For many, there is still pain in our hearts that keeps us in bondage. The good news is Jesus has provided a solution for this as well! Freedom is available, but few have been taught how to break free.

Consider that we will have our memories in Heaven. Yet, there is no pain in Heaven, so we will have our memories, but there will be no painful memories attached to our memories. Jesus said that life should be *on earth as it is in Heaven.* If it is to be on earth as it is in Heaven, then we can have the pain of our memories removed here on earth. We do not have to wait until Heaven to have our memories healed of pain. In fact, Jesus will transform painful experiences from hindrances into testimonies. There is no need to wait until Heaven; we can have our memories changed right now!

Many books have been written on the subject of how to heal memories and bring health to our emotional lives. Unfortunately many of these books complicate the process of healing until we are left reading something the size of a telephone book. These complex models cannot be found in the ministry of Jesus; therefore, I do not want them. What *is* found in the ministry of Jesus is simply forgiving others. Forgiveness is the profound truth that brings healing to the heart, mind, and memories.

If we will not deal with the pain in our memories, we leave ourselves vulnerable to spiritual attack. Apostle Paul spoke of the condition of our hearts when he said, *"Do not give the devil a foothold"* (Eph. 4:27). The picture here is of your heart as a rock-face cliff with places for a climber to grasp onto. When we allow unforgiveness to dwell in our hearts, we allow satan a place to grasp and hang onto us.

Jesus is the example for all life; therefore, we find by looking at His life that He gave no footholds for satan to grasp Him. *"I will not speak with you much longer, for the prince of this world is coming. He has no hold on Me"* (John 14:30). I imagine the clean perfection of Jesus' heart as a rock-faced cliff that has been sanded perfectly smooth and covered with petroleum jelly just for good measure.

Jesus never allowed unforgiveness to take hold or fester in His heart. He kept His heart safe by always forgiving immediately and thoroughly. One of the best examples is when, in the middle of being crucified, He chose to take a moment and release forgiveness. *"Father, forgive them, for they do not know what they are doing"* (Luke 23:34). In the midst of all that pain, He did not allow unforgiveness to creep into His heart.

Many people often claim that they have forgiven, yet if there is still pain in the memory, then there is still more forgiveness needed. From John 14:30, we see that Jesus had no place of pain, unforgiveness, or offense in His heart. Therefore, satan had no hold in His life.

Four Steps to Healing

For memories with painful emotions attached to them (such as shame, anger, fear, or hatred), use this simple four-step process to pray through those memories and remove the footholds from your heart.

1. Forgive the offender in detail for what was done.

2. Repent for allowing unforgiveness in your heart.

Step two is much larger than most people realize at first. At some point, each of us has to take responsibility for our own thoughts and feelings. Many Christians have allowed the sins of bitterness, resentment, fear, condemnation, and hatred to fester in their hearts. We must realize that we don't just need to forgive others, but God also requires that *we repent* for the putrid resentments in our own souls. Yes, our offender hurt us, but we were the ones who chose to hold onto rather than forgive the offense.

3.   Command the lies of the past and the demonic to be silent.

John 10:5 says, *"They will never follow a stranger; in fact, they will run away from him because they do not recognize a stranger's voice."* Because we are in Christ and our past is not, our past represents the voice of a stranger. Even though it seems familiar, it is actually a lie because God says that past no longer exists. So we must command the voice of the past and of the demonic to be silent.

4.   Ask the Holy Spirit to speak His truth into your heart about that memory.

You may hear a word, a sentence, or perhaps see a picture in your mind. God speaks to people in many different ways. Sometimes when you finish one prayer, the Lord will speak to you about another memory that has pain in it, so you can continue your healing process. Many times multiple prayers are needed to bring total healing to the affected memories. Pain is an excellent guidepost; keep praying until all the pain has been removed.

Write down what you hear the Holy Spirit say to your heart regarding each memory. You will be blessed to be able to go back and read that again in the future. Repeat the four steps for each memory that has pain and unforgiveness in it.

Begin your four-step process by creating a list. Ask the Holy Spirit to convict your heart of where there is hurt or unforgiveness. Now begin your list with categories such as: Father, Mother, Brother, Sister, Employer, Teacher, Pastor, Babysitter, Friends, Spouse, Boy/Girlfriends, and so forth.

Under each category, write briefly the memories that still carry pain. Once you have completed your list, begin the four-step process with each memory. I suggest even subcategorizing with other groupings such as sexual, verbal, or physical abuse.

Here is a practical example to follow:

I choose to forgive _____ *(insert name) for what he/she did (or said) to me (be specific).*

I repent for holding unforgiveness toward _____ *(insert name); I choose to release him/her of their debt to me right now. They owe me nothing. I repent for believing the lie that I* _____.

I command the voice of the enemy to be silent. I will not allow you to speak to me through this memory any longer.

Holy Spirit, please tell me Your truth about this memory.

Now listen to the Holy Spirit.

When I used this four-step process, I spent a week writing my list. Then I went to the local park and sat at a picnic table for two solid hours by myself and prayed through item after item on my list. When I picked up my list to continue after a lunch break, I was surprised to notice a marked difference between the items I had prayed through and the ones I had not yet prayed through. I felt nothing when I looked at the ones I had prayed through; no regret, no pain, and no shame. But I could feel a sting of emotions when I looked at the ones I had not yet prayed through. That definitely motivated me to finish my list.

A remarkable thing happened when I reached the bottom of my prayer list. I felt as though a large invisible hand lifted off me. This was the feeling associated with all the pressure and power of those memories that compelled me to act and think in certain ways. I actually had a hard time standing at first when that pressure lifted off because I felt lighter and freer than ever before.

As the week went on, I realized that I was free of the compulsions toward which my memories had been pushing me. Then the Holy Spirit told me that I would now for the first time begin to understand what true self-control is, because I had been under the control of my painful memories for so long that I had no idea what self-control looked like.

It is time for you to get free from the pain and lies that hold you in bondage. I encourage you to take your time creating a detailed list, and do not rush through the four-step prayer process. It took years to accumulate those painful memories; you can take a few days to heal them.

CONCLUSION

Normal Christians are not filled with insecurity about their relationship with God. They know that they have been fully forgiven and that if they commit a sin, they can immediately receive cleansing from the blood of Jesus sprinkled on their consciences. There is no concern about whether God will forgive or not, because that issue was settled when God forgave all sin through the death of Jesus. Normal Christians are the most peaceful, confident, calm, tranquil, and secure individuals in the world because they know that they are clean, forgiven, and free of their debt of sin. Normal Christians have no condemnation, are full of forgiveness, have a clean conscience, and carry no painful memories. Therefore, they walk in confidence and freedom every day.

ACTIVATION I

1. Ask the Holy Spirit to convict you of sin (see John 16:7-8).

2. Repent; ask the Spirit to apply the blood of Jesus to your defiled conscience (see Heb. 10:22).

3. Ask the Spirit to remind you of your tremendous righteousness in Christ (see Rom. 5:17).

4. Let the Spirit redirect your heart toward retribution on the demonic (see Rom. 16:19).

ACTIVATION 2

Create your painful memories list.

Use the four-step process in detail upon each memory.

Write down a record of what the Holy Spirit says or shows you regarding each memory. (It can be very helpful to have another person read this chapter, then lead you in prayer through the four steps of processing your memories.)

ACKNOWLEDGMENTS

Thank you to Dan Mohler and Todd White. I don't know any two men who exemplify living out the righteousness of Christ like you do. Continue to shine like stars in the darkness until the whole world is filled with His marvelous light.

ENDNOTE

1. Watchman Nee, *The Life that Wins* (New York: Christian Fellowship Pulishers, 1986), 26.

CHAPTER SIX

THE LAND OF
WIMPY PRAYERS

*Immature or soulish Christians come into shaky situations praying,
"If it be your will Lord." Whereas, the Spirit-led Christian, prays,
"Father, I ask you to do this." There's a world of difference in the faith
levels of those two prayers. A soulish Christian will pray in hope; a
spirit Christian will pray in faith.* —Graham Cooke[1]

THE POWER OF THE NAME

O nce upon a time in a kingdom not so far away, there was a king named
Edmond. He was a good and kind ruler, beloved of all his subjects. His
kingdom was vast and covered many lands and peoples. His people lived
knowing that their king loved them and cared for their welfare. However,
there was also an evil man named Lou who lived within the kingdom, and his
greatest desire was to disrupt the peace that King Edmond had established.
Lou would attack the villagers, cause calamity, murder, steal, and destroy
crops and livestock. Lou knew that he was no match for King Edmond
directly, but he could hurt the heart of the king by harming his dear subjects.

One day King Edmond determined to empower his people to stand up to Lou, so he gave them the greatest weapon a king can possibly give, the power of his name. This meant that every attack on one of King Edmond's subjects was the same as a direct attack against the king himself. This also meant that each lowly subject had the full authority to command and direct the king's armies to fight Lou, whenever and wherever needed.

At first this delegated authority worked wonderfully, and Lou was driven back farther and farther every day. Over time, however, many of those in the kingdom forgot what it meant to be given the king's name. They no longer understood how to use this weapon to protect their communities and destroy the work of Lou.

Every once in a great while, a servant would arise from what seemed like nowhere with an understanding of using the king's name to powerfully rout Lou's current schemes. These individuals would revive the power of delegated authority. They were given the name *revivalists*. But the revivalists were discouraged by this name, because they desired to see all the subjects rise up and take back the weapon of the king's name. The power of the name was meant to be used by all people rather than by a select few. To this very day, nobody knows how this story ends. Will the subjects continue to live powerless lives of defeat while hoping that a revivalist will arise and perhaps save them? Will Lou continue to plunder and destroy without any resistance rising up against him? Or will the villagers learn again how to use the power of delegated authority that they have been given to defeat Lou?

This story represents the present state of prayer in the modern Church. Most Christians have approached prayer with the idea that we must beg our King to give us what we need. But King Jesus has given us His name and expects us to use this authority to defeat the devil and spread the peace of His Kingdom far and wide.

> *And I will do whatever you ask **in My name**, so that the Son may bring glory to the Father. You may ask Me for anything **in My name**, and I will do it* (John 14:13-14).

You did not choose Me, but I chose you and appointed you to go and bear fruit—fruit that will last. Then the Father will give you whatever you ask in My name (John 15:16).

This powerful promise has been turned into a vain repetition by the modern Church. Typically it is used as a signal that the prayer being prayed is finished, "In Jesus' name, amen." It has been approached as a magic formula of sorts—say it at the end of a prayer to make it official. We must regain an understanding of the power of His name and how it is to be used. Let's look closely at the power of names and what it means to pray in someone's name.

WHAT'S IN A NAME?

To the typical person in the 21st century, the following passage is just a long, boring genealogy, most likely to be skipped while reading. But to a Hebrew in ancient Israel, this passage is actually a powerful prophecy about the coming Messiah—Jesus the Christ.

*This is the family tree of the human race: When God created the human race, he made it godlike, with a nature akin to God. He created both male and female and blessed them, the whole human race. When **Adam** was 130 years old, he had a son who was just like him, his very spirit and image, and named him Seth. After the birth of Seth, Adam lived another 800 years, having more sons and daughters. Adam lived a total of 930 years. And he died.*

*When **Seth** was 105 years old, he had Enosh. After Seth had Enosh, he lived another 807 years, having more sons and daughters. Seth lived a total of 912 years. And he died. When **Enosh** was ninety years old, he had Kenan. After he had Kenan, he lived another 815 years, having more sons and daughters. Enosh lived a total of 905 years. And he died. When **Kenan** was seventy years old, he had Mahalalel. After he had **Mahalalel**, he lived another*

840 years, having more sons and daughters. Kenan lived a total of 910 years. And he died. When Mahalalel was sixty-five years old, he had Jared. After he had Jared, he lived another 830 years, having more sons and daughters. Mahalalel lived a total of 895 years. And he died.

*When **Jared** was 162 years old, he had Enoch. After he had Enoch, he lived another 800 years, having more sons and daughters. Jared lived a total of 962 years. And he died. When **Enoch** was sixty-five years old, he had Methuselah. Enoch walked steadily with God. After he had Methuselah, he lived another 300 years, having more sons and daughters. Enoch lived a total of 365 years. Enoch walked steadily with God. And then one day he was simply gone: God took him. When **Methuselah** was 187 years old, he had Lamech. After he had Lamech, he lived another 782 years. Methuselah lived a total of 969 years. And he died.*

*When **Lamech** was 182 years old, he had a son. He named him Noah, saying, "This one will give us a break from the hard work of farming the ground that God cursed." After Lamech had **Noah**, he lived another 595 years, having more sons and daughters. Lamech lived a total of 777 years. And he died* (Genesis 5:1-31 MSG).

In Hebrew culture, names are not merely labels for differentiating objects and persons. Names also declare the nature of a thing. For example, in this Genesis 5 passage, there are ten names listed. Each name has a meaning, and when these ten meanings are lined up, a clear prophecy is declared about the Son of God.

TEN NAMES AND MEANINGS IN GENESIS 5

1. Adam—Man

2. Seth—Appointed

3. Enosh—Mortal

4. Kenan—Sorrow

5. Mahalalel—The Blessed God

6. Jared—To come down

7. Enoch—Teaching

8. Methuselah—His death shall bring

9. Lamech—The weary

10. Noah—Rest

To an ancient Hebrew reading this genealogy, the ten names and their meanings give a profound prophecy about the coming Messiah. They read that He would be a *Man Appointed Mortal Sorrow,* that He would actually be *The Blessed God* who would *Come Down Teaching,* and finally that *His Death Shall Bring the Weary Rest.* Much is missed by modern Christians when we do not look closely at the power of the meaning of names in the Bible.

An interesting point about Methuselah is that his name means "his death shall bring." Did you know that he died the exact same year that the flood came? His whole life he must have wondered what his death would bring, and people must have speculated, "What is his death going to bring?" Perhaps his grandson, Noah, was thinking, "God told me He would destroy the whole world. And you are the oldest guy I know, and your death is said to bring something. Maybe I should hurry and finish this because you could die any day now."

At the end of his life, Methuselah might have been walking around saying, "When are you going to finish the ark? I want to die and go to Heaven. Please finish it now!" Noah's name means "rest." When you consider that he created an ark that simply floated through a global storm, *rest* is a good word to characterize his life.

NAMES REVEAL CHARACTER

Names are not merely labels; they are creative, they declare destiny, and they pronounce the nature of a person or thing. Throughout the Bible, God has revealed His names to us. Each name reveals something of who He is as a person. Here are eight examples of the names God shared with us in the Bible.

1. El-Shaddai—The Almighty God (see Gen. 17:1-2)

2. Jehovah-Jireh—The Lord our Provider (see Gen. 22:14)

3. Jehovah-Rapha—The Lord our Healer (see Exod. 15:22-26)

4. Jehovah-Tsidqenu—The Lord our Righteousness (see Jer. 33:16)

5. Jehovah-Nissi—The Lord is Conqueror (see Exod. 17:15)

6. Jehovah-Shalom—The Lord our Peace (see Judg. 6:24)

7. Jehovah-Shammah—The Lord is With You (see Ezek. 48:35)

8. Jehovah-Sabaoth—The Lord of Hosts (see Rom. 9:29)

These are not labels for God. This is not like calling God "Steve" or "Tim." These names are intended to reveal to humankind the nature of God as a person. As a person God is a Provider, He is a Healer, He is a Commander of hosts of angels. Each name reveals who He is. The word *Jehovah* can be understood as self-revealing. So when it says Jehovah-Rapha, it generally means, "God, who has revealed Himself to us as the Healer."

It is interesting to see the timing and circumstances of God revealing His names in the Word. One of the earliest names He gave was in Exodus 15:26, *"I am the Lord who heals you"* (Jehovah-Rapha). In context, the Hebrews were living in Egypt, and they were surrounded by diseases and plagues. They saw all of the plagues that were upon the Egyptians. God spoke to His people and said, *"I am the Lord who heals you. I will protect you and keep you from all the diseases of the Egyptians."*

God is not saying, "Hey, maybe you should call Me Rapha today or maybe you should call Me Nissi today." He is not just giving us several labels so that we can pick and choose what we want. He says, "No, this is who I am. If you need Jehovah-Rapha, Jehovah-Rapha's here for you. If you need Jehovah-Nissi, Jehovah-Nissi's here for you. If you need Jehovah-Jireh, I am your Jehovah-Jireh." He is revealing His character in each one of those names. They identify who He is.

Names represent the nature and character of a person. In fact, names are so significant that there are three instances in Scripture where God chose to change a person's name to put that person on the path to his or her calling.

Jacob

The name Jacob means "supplanter or deceiver." Jacob grew up being called a liar, and it became an ingrained part of his personality. He walked around his whole life living according to his calling and his name. He tricked his father, his brother, and his uncle Laban each on separate occasions. But let's jump ahead to the day when Jacob had an encounter with God and received a new name.

> *So Jacob was left alone, and a Man wrestled with him till daybreak. When the Man saw that He could not overpower him, He touched the socket of Jacob's hip so that his hip was wrenched as he wrestled with the Man. Then the Man said, "Let Me go, for it is daybreak. But Jacob replied, "I will not let You go unless You bless me." The Man asked him, "What is your name?" "Jacob,"* he answered. *Then the Man said, "Your name will no longer be Jacob* [liar], *but Israel* [prince with God], *because you have*

struggled with God and with men and have overcome" (Genesis 32:24-28).

We receive further insight into this story from Hosea 12:2-4:

The LORD has a charge to bring against Judah; He will punish Jacob according to his ways and repay him according to his deeds. In the womb he grasped at his brother's heel; as a man he strug-gled with God. He struggled with the Angel and overcame Him; **he wept and begged for His favor.** *He found Him at Bethel and talked with Him there."*

Jacob fought the Angel until he broke down weeping. He then demanded a blessing from his opponent.

By asking the question, "What is your name?" the angel is not asking for the label that Jacob is known by, but rather how Jacob views himself as a person. Jacob responds with the deep realization, "I am a liar, deceiver, sup-planter; this is who I am." In that moment of realization and repentance, the angel responds with a new name and a new nature for Jacob: You are no longer Jacob; you are now Israel. You are no longer a liar; now you are a prince with God. What the angel said is not just a new label for Jacob. He changed his nature, his calling, and his destiny. God does the same thing for us, spiritually, when we repent of sins.

ABRAM AND SARAI

The name Abram means "exalted father," yet he was an old man with no children. One day God appeared to Abram and told him, *"No longer will you be called Abram; your name will be Abraham, for I have made you a father of many nations"* (Gen. 17:5). This would be rather strange, even for someone with a few children, but extremely weird for Abram, whose wife was barren.

Abram was married to a woman named Sarai, which translates to "con-tentious one." Clearly she was no happy camper! God had a solution for her problem as well. *"God also said to Abraham, 'As for Sarai your wife, you are no longer to call her Sarai; her name will be Sarah'"* (Gen. 17:15). He changes her name to Sarah, which means, "princess of multitudes." So Sarai goes from being a contentious wife to being a princess. Good deal, and I bet no one was happier about this change than Abraham!

At this point in the story, God has renamed them both and given them a prophecy about being the mother and father of many nations. God has given them a new nature, calling, and destiny contained within these new names. As they begin to call each other by these new names, they begin to call forth their new destiny. Later in the story, they give birth to Isaac, and their prophecy is fulfilled as they become the parents of the Jewish people. This union eventually brings forth Jesus, who welcomes all nations into His family and makes Abraham the father of many nations (see Gal. 3:16).

SIMON

Jumping from the Book of Genesis to the New Testament, we find that even Jesus changed someone's name. *"Then Andrew brought Simon to meet Jesus. Looking intently at Simon, Jesus said, 'Your name is Simon, son of John— but you will be called Cephas'* (which means Peter)" (John 1:42 NLT). The name Simon means "broken reed," and Jesus determined that He was not going to walk around calling Simon a broken reed for the next three and a half years. Jesus says that Simon would be called Cephas (Peter), which means "a stone." The prophetic nature of God speaks to broken people like Simon and infuses new strength into them. (Another example of how God speaks strength into broken people is how God spoke to the coward Gideon and declared him to be a mighty man of valor in Judges 6:11-12.)

As Jesus interacted with Peter, He always called him up to a higher standard, drawing the greatness out of him. Jesus told Peter that he was a rock and that *"on this rock I will build My church..."* (Matt. 16:18). Jesus interacted with him not as a broken reed. He called him according to his destiny.

At this point you may be wishing that God would give you a new name. The truth is, God *does* have a new name for you! *"...I will also give him a white stone with a new name written on it, known only to him who receives it"* (Rev. 2:17). God actually has a new name for each one of us. We may not know what it is yet, but we are not bound by the names of our old nature that try to cling to us: sinner, thief, failure, loser, promiscuous, and the like. We are not given our white stone with a new name on it until we arrive in Heaven, but during our time on earth, Jesus gave us His name to use. This is an incredible privilege. Let us now look closely to understand the amazing benefits of this gift.

The Promise of the Name

The day of His crucifixion was drawing close, and Jesus was preparing His disciples for His departure. He told them many things to get them ready for the difficult process ahead, but one of the most assuring things that He gave them was complete authority in prayer. He wanted them to be completely filled with joy, and one way that would happen is by having their prayers answered.

> *In that day you will no longer ask Me anything. I tell you the truth, My Father will give you whatever you ask in My name. Until now you have not asked for anything in My name. Ask and you will receive, and your joy will be complete* (John 16:23-24).

> *In that day you will ask in My name. I am not saying that I will ask the Father on your behalf* (John 16:26).

Jesus put very specific time restraints upon the promise of His name. Clearly this was a promise that, in the future, followers of Jesus would have access to use His name. So do we currently have access to Jesus' name, and if so, when did we receive it?

*Your attitude should be the same as that of Christ Jesus: Who, being in very nature God, did not consider equality with God something to be grasped, but made Himself nothing, taking the very nature of a servant, being made in human likeness. And being found in appearance as a man, He humbled himself and became obedient to death—even death on a cross! Therefore God exalted Him to the highest place and gave Him **the name** that is **above every name**, that at **the name of Jesus** every knee should bow, in heaven and on earth and under the earth, and every tongue confess that Jesus Christ is Lord, to the glory of God the Father* (Philippians 2:5-11).

When Jesus gave them the promise of the future use of His name, it was just before the end of His earthly life. Through Jesus' death and resurrection, He received the name above all other names. His name was granted the highest authority in the universe. Jesus didn't give us His name before the cross because He wanted us to receive the full value of His name. He had to complete His mission so that when we received His name it would contain all the authority that He wanted us to have.

IN THE *BEING* OF JESUS

God has promised us the authority to use the name of Jesus. So how do we operate within this promise? As we have learned, names are not merely labels. They declare the nature and character of the person. Another way to understand this would be to replace the word *name* with the word *being*. For example, in the Lord's Prayer of Matthew 6:9, *"Our Father in heaven, hallowed* [holy] *be Your name."* This verse is not saying that the labels by which we call God are holy labels. This becomes clear when we replace the word *name* with the word *being. Our Father in heaven, hallowed be Your **being**.* Essentially, *holy* is who God *is* as a person. Because names declare who a person is, we can use the words *name* and *being* interchangeably. Here is another example where we see this:

But these are written that you may believe that Jesus is the Christ, the Son of God, and that by believing you may have life in His name (John 20:31).

This verse makes even more sense by reading it this way, *"...that by believing you may have life in His **being**."*

Jesus has so connected us to His name that we should look more closely at what He said to Paul on the road to Damascus.

As he neared Damascus on his journey, suddenly a light from heaven flashed around him. He fell to the ground and heard a voice say to him, "Saul, Saul, why do you persecute Me?" "Who are You, Lord?" Saul asked. "I am Jesus, whom you are persecuting," He replied (Acts 9:3-5).

How can an earthly person, Saul, with a letter from the high priest, persecute Jesus of Nazareth, who sits in Heaven at the right hand of God? The connection between body and head is so strong that an attack on the delegated authority of the body is an attack on the head, Jesus.

This is the reason the Lord did not say to Saul, "Why do you persecute My people?" or "Why do you persecute My Church?" Instead He said, "Why do you persecute Me?" Because we stand in His *name*, in His *being*—as His representatives, an attack upon us is an attack upon Him.

Therefore, to "pray in the name of Jesus" becomes clearer when we make the following substitution: "Praying in the being of Jesus."

AMBASSADORS

To truly pray in the name of Jesus is to understand your position of delegated authority. You have been commissioned as an ambassador upon the earth. As the apostle Paul wrote, *"We are, therefore Christ's ambassadors, as though God were making His appeal through us. We implore you on Christ's behalf; Be reconciled to God"* (2 Cor. 5:20).

As an ambassador, you stand in delegated authority. When you rebuke a demon, it is as if Jesus is rebuking that demon; when you rebuke a sickness, it is as if Jesus is rebuking that sickness—that is the power of delegated authority.

To give someone the right to use *your name* is to give them *your authority*. That person is authorized to speak as your representative. Presently, Jesus is sitting at the right hand of the Father, waiting while His ambassadors (the Church) put His enemies under His feet (see Heb. 10:12-13).

As ambassadors, our priority is bringing alignment between Heaven and earth. Jesus said that we are to pray that it would be on earth as it is in Heaven (see Matt. 6:10). In Heaven there is no sickness, no pain, no poverty, no divorce, no broken homes, no death. In Heaven there is total peace, love, and joy. Therefore, as an ambassador of Heaven, these are the things that we pray into our surroundings.

It is time to move away from wimpy, weak-kneed, milk-toast, namby-pamby prayers like, *"God, if it is Your will, would You please consider doing such and such?"* Ambassadors direct their authority toward the problem and demand results. I am not saying that we make demands of God, but that we aim our authority at the problem. For example, "Lazarus come forth!" or "Lame man rise and walk!" or "Demon come out!" "Storm be calm!" Like Jesus, ambassadors use their authority to address problems directly.

When you pray in the *being* of Jesus, you must be obeyed by demons, sickness, death, and circumstances as if Jesus Himself were commanding those obstacles. I, Jonathan Welton, have no authority in my name, apart from Jesus. In the natural, I am not a king, but as an ambassador of Heaven, I operate in the authority of the King of kings. When I am praying, I am standing inside the being of Jesus, because that is where I find my authority.

The Church has understood select portions of her identity, but she must grasp her ambassadorship to grasp authority in prayer. She must step beyond her current revelation of prayer to understand that authority comes from identity and her identity is *in Christ*.

Praying With Authority

As Peter and John were on their way to temple on the Sabbath, a man who could not walk was begging for money by the gate. They both looked at the beggar and exercised their authority as God's representatives.

> ...*Then Peter said, "Look at us!" So the man gave them his attention, expecting to get something from them. Then Peter said, "Silver or gold I do not have, but what I have I give you. In the name of Jesus Christ of Nazareth, walk"* (Acts 3:4-6).

As a result of this healing on the Sabbath, Peter and John were brought before the Pharisees. The Pharisees asked them, *"By what power or what name did you do this?"* (Acts 4:7b). Notice that the Hebrew culture understood the power of ambassadorial authority; this is why they asked, "*in what name did you do this?"* They are actually asking, "Who gave you the authority to overrule Sabbath law and heal someone?" I am sure that the Pharisees had an inkling that these were disciples of Jesus, because He was constantly going against their rules by healing on the Sabbath.

Notice how the apostle used the name of Jesus. He did not pray, "Lord if it is Your will, please consider healing this lame man." Instead, Peter forcefully grabbed the man's attention and declared, *In the name of Jesus, walk!* To paraphrase for clarity, I put it this way, "Mr. lame man, I am an ambassador of Heaven, here with the authority to declare things as if Jesus were declaring them, and I say, Get up and walk!"

Hostile Territory

This planet we inhabit is hostile territory. When Adam and Eve ate of the Tree of the Knowledge of Good and Evil, they released death into the world, and this has affected us all. Yet through Christ, Christians have been given eternal life and authority as ambassadors to bring Heaven and earth back into alignment. This does not mean that we will not encounter resistance. Demons, sickness, death, and poverty do not want to submit to our authority. They will resist with all their might, but we must stand and impose Heaven's rule—not by lobbying and legislation, but through prayer with authority.

Once you grasp this, the tone of your prayer life shifts from wimpy to aggressive. Your prayers move from begging God to do something for you, to standing as His representative and commanding change to occur in the earth.

That is where Isaiah 55 comes in:

> *As the rain and the snow come down from heaven, and do not return to it without watering the earth and making it bud and flourish, so that it yields seed for the sower and bread for the eater, so is my word that goes out from My mouth: It will not return to Me empty, but will accomplish what I desire and achieve the purpose for which I sent it* (Isaiah 55:10-11).

As ambassadors, we speak our prayers with authority and expect results to occur. We have been placed in many environments to affect them for the Kingdom of Heaven: family, business, church, the arts, media, the government, and so forth. We can use our authority to release God's answers into earth's problems.

Your words, according to Isaiah 55, change what they are being spoken over. As the next two verses show, the result of declaring over your environment is that you affect it so much that it responds to you. Isaiah says that the mountains will burst into song, trees will clap their hands, and the produce of the ground will be changed.

> *You will go out in joy and be led forth in peace; the mountains and hills will burst into song before you, and all the trees of the field will clap their hands. Instead of the thorn bush will grow the pine tree, and instead of briers the myrtle will grow. This will*

be for the LORD's renown, for an everlasting sign, which will not be destroyed (Isaiah 55:12-13).

Our words and prayers shift environments. As His representatives in the earth, God has given us tremendous responsibility. To accomplish these shifts, He equipped us with the greatest authority in the universe, the name of Jesus.

> *…God exalted Him to the highest place and gave Him **the name** that is **above every name**, that at **the name of Jesus** every knee should bow, in heaven and on earth and under the earth, and every tongue confess that Jesus Christ is Lord, to the glory of God the Father* (Philippians 2:9-11).

ACTIVATION

What in your environment needs to come into alignment with Heaven's best: physical ailments, financial issues, your marriage, your children, your church, close friends, your employer and co-workers, and so forth. Speak over each of these with authority as Heaven's ambassador.

ACKNOWLEDGMENT

To Roger Hart. When your friend prayed with authority in the name of Jesus, it cured you of thyroid cancer. Now you have learned how to pray with this same authority. When I need prayer, you are one of the first I seek. You have been like a David to this Jonathan. I love you so much.

ENDNOTE

1. Graham Cooke, *Drawing Close* (Ada, MI: Cosen Books, 2005), 36.

CHAPTER SEVEN

WOMEN RISING

Oh, that the ministers of religion would search the original records of God's Word in order to discover whether the general notions of society are not wrong on this subject, and whether God really intended woman to bury her gifts and talents, as she now does.
—Catherine Booth, Cofounder of the Salvation Army

Many years before the time of King David, Israel was enslaved by the Canaanites. The Israelites had once again walked away from the Lord and as happened so many times during that era, they were enslaved again. Deborah the prophetess was the recognized national leader among the Hebrews during that time.

The Lord directed Deborah to bring Israel out of slavery. Deborah prophesied to a man named Barak that He was to gather a volunteer army of ten thousand men to fight for freedom. She also provided his battle strategy and assured him of victory. In that moment, Barak, if he were like most men, might have been pondering what being the hero of the entire nation would be like, but he had a different thought. Barak realized he was being given a tremendous honor by this prophetic word. Although Barak may have been tempted to keep the honor of this victory for himself and the men of the army, he chose instead to honor Deborah in return.

Barak said to her, "If you go with me, I will go; but if you don't go with me, I won't go."

"Very well," Deborah said. "I will go with you." "But because of the way you are going about this, the honor will not be yours, for the Lord will hand Sisera [the enemy general] *over to a woman..."* (Judges 4:8-9).

Barak had no obligation to honor Deborah; he could have kept the honor for himself and his men, but he chose to share the honor with Deborah. By doing so, he passed the honor to all women. Deborah did not keep the honor to herself; she went on to declare that Barak would not get the honor and neither would she; rather, the honor would go to a no-name woman. By the divine exchange that takes place between Deborah and Barak, we see a divine order of empowerment between the genders.

Presently, the Church is full of wonderful Deborah's who have been honoring men for many years. It is time for a company of Barak's to rise up—humble and confident men who are not willing to keep the honor of leadership to themselves, men who will empower women to step into their call and destiny.

Many have been asking the Lord, "Where are the Deborah's?" A better prayer would be, "Lord, raise up men as a Barak company!"

WHERE IT ALL BEGAN

From the very beginning of humanity there has always been a battle for dominance between the sexes. Let us go back and see where it all started.

Now the serpent was more crafty than any of the wild animals the LORD God had made. He said to the woman, "Did God really say, 'You must not eat from any tree in the garden'?" The woman said to the serpent, "We may eat fruit from the trees in the garden, but God did say, 'You must not eat fruit from the tree that is in the middle of the garden, and you must not touch it, or you will die.'"

"You will not surely die," the serpent said to the woman. "For God knows that when you eat of it your eyes will be opened, and you will be like God, knowing good and evil." When the woman saw that the fruit of the tree was good for food and pleasing to the eye, and also desirable for gaining wisdom, she took some and ate it. She also gave some to her husband, who was with her, and he ate it. Then the eyes of both of them were opened, and they realized they were naked; so they sewed fig leaves together and made coverings for themselves.

Then the man and his wife heard the sound of the LORD God as He was walking in the garden in the cool of the day, and they hid from the LORD God among the trees of the garden. But the LORD God called to the man, "Where are you?" He answered, "I heard You in the garden, and I was afraid because I was naked; so I hid." And He said, "Who told you that you were naked? Have you eaten from the tree that I commanded you not to eat from?" The man said, "The woman You put here with me—she gave me some fruit from the tree, and I ate it." Then the LORD God said to the woman, "What is this you have done?" The woman said, "The serpent deceived me, and I ate" (Genesis 3:1-13).

After this, God placed a curse upon the serpent, a curse upon the woman, and a curse upon the ground that Adam would be tending. The curse that was placed upon the woman is the curse that caused the gender war. What was the curse upon the woman?

To the woman He said, "I will greatly increase your pains in childbearing; with pain you will give birth to children. **Your desire will be for your husband, and he will rule over you"** (Genesis 3:16).

This phrasing works as a statement of action and reaction. Because the woman "desires" her husband, he will "rule over" her. Yet this does not make much sense as a curse. Why should a woman's desire for her husband cause him to dominate her? Most men would gladly accept their wife's desires for them, causing them to treat her more gently rather than roughly, as is implied in this verse. How are we to understand this?

The key is in the word "desire," translated from the Hebrew *tesuqah*, which occurs only three times in the Old Testament. It is best understood through its usage in Genesis 4:7 (NKJV), which shows another side, that of a desire to overcome or defeat another: "[Sin's] *desire is for you, but you should rule over it."*

Thus, God is saying that a woman's desire will be to gain the upper hand over her husband, but because she is the weaker vessel, her husband will put her down by force, if need be. The curse is essentially that women will lose the battle of the sexes. History bears this out. Until the advent of women's rights movements, women were virtually their husband's property, treated as heir-producing machines, given little freedom, and forced to serve their husband's every whim. In many cultures, men bought and sold women like cattle. Some cultures maintain this custom even today. In fact, women's rights have only existed in mainstream culture since Susan B. Anthony and the Suffrage movement of the 1920s.[1]

Adam Names the Woman

After God had released the curses for rebellion, including the subjugation of woman, Adam named his wife. Until this point in the story (see Gen. 1-3:19), his wife was only referred to as *the woman,* but now Adam doles out a name for her. And so, *the woman* becomes *Eve.* This may seem small and insignificant, but if we consider that Adam and *the woman* had walked as equals before the curse, this is actually a profound detail. *"Adam named his wife Eve, because she would become the mother of all the living"* (Gen. 3:20).

Previously, Adam had been given dominion in Genesis 1:28 to rule over all the animals, birds, and fish; but he did not rule over woman until the curse occurred. When the woman received the curse of subjugation, Adam named her in the same manner that he had named all the animals of the garden (see Gen. 2:19-20). By naming *the woman,* Adam took dominion over *Eve* in the same way that he took dominion over the animals. And so the curse was applied and enacted. God called this a curse because He never desired for them to be unequal. It was not God's intention, but rather a result of sin. In fact, in the story of Noah, we find that God worked to bring restoration of equality in the Old Testament.

Noah and His Sons

By the time we get to Genesis 6:5-7, we find that the earth had become wicked. We learn of God's plan to wipe out the first creation with a worldwide flood and start again with the only righteous people on earth, Noah and his family. Skipping ahead in the story, God had Noah build an ark in preparation for the flood.

And Noah and his sons and his wife and his sons' wives entered the ark to escape the waters of the flood (Genesis 7:7).

*On that very day **Noah and his sons**, Shem, Ham and Japheth, together with **his wife and the wives of his three sons**, entered the ark* (Genesis 7:13).

Sometimes it can seem like the Bible provides us with odd details, but it is surprising how much can be contained in a small statement like the preceding verses. Looking at these two verses you can see that Noah and the other men went into the Ark first, and then the women followed. Once the flood was over, God gave Noah very specific directions as to how to exit the ark. *"Then God said to Noah, 'Come out of the ark, **you and your wife and your sons and their wives'"** (Gen. 8:15-16).

God intended to bring the eight of them out of the ark as couples walking in unity and equality. He was trying to start the planet over with at least a partial redemption of gender equality. Unfortunately, we read that Noah disobeyed the Lord's specific instructions. *"So Noah came out, together with his sons and his wife and his sons' wives"* (Gen. 8:18).

We see from this that God desired to restore women, but man's disobedience got in the way. Not much progression in the restoration of equality took place between the Garden of Eden and when Jesus came upon the scene 4,000 years later. As we will see though, what Jesus accomplished changed everything.

Jesus, the Ultimate Redeemer

In the Garden of Eden, there was equality between men and women. In Heaven, there will be no curses (see Rev. 22:3), which means that women will be fully restored. Currently, we live in a timeline between these two curseless realities, the Garden of Eden and Heaven. When Jesus entered this timeline where men and women live on earth under the curses, He came to bring us freedom. Jesus came to bring the future reality of Heaven into our present. He even passed this commission to His Church when He told us to bring Heaven (future) into earth (present).

*This, then, is how you should pray, "Our Father in heaven, hallowed be Your name, Your kingdom come, **Your will be done on earth as it is in heaven"** (Matthew 6:9-10).*

Because of what Jesus accomplished on the cross, freeing humanity from the power of the curse, we do not have to wait until Heaven for the curse to be removed. In fact, according to Paul, Jesus has changed the current timeline so that we do not dwell under gender, economic, or racial curses any longer.

You are all sons of God through faith in Christ Jesus, for all of you who were baptized into Christ have clothed yourselves with Christ. There is neither Jew nor Greek, slave nor free, male nor female, for you are all one in Christ Jesus (Galatians 3:26-28).

Jesus came to redeem all humanity from every curse, including the curses that were incurred by Adam and Eve in Genesis 3. Because we have been placed inside of Christ and Christ has been placed inside of us, it doesn't matter whether we are Jews, slaves, females, or Greeks—all in Christ are equal. God's perspective, when He looks at individuals in His Church, is that He is not looking at male and female, African or European, bank owner or welfare recipient—He is looking at the heart and seeing Christ.

This is what God was trying to explain to the prophet Samuel when he was searching for the next king of Israel. *"Man looks at the outward appearance, but the LORD looks at the heart"* (1 Sam. 16:7b). The Lord's perspective is different from ours. Consider that God has never been under any curse; therefore, He does not treat us according to the curses. The Genesis 3 curse never said that women were going to be accursed of God and, therefore, could not be used for leadership. The curse only changed the way that men and women would interact, not the way that God would interact with women.

God has always looked not at the outward, but at the heart of the believer, which is where Jesus is dwelling. So when God looks at a believer, it does not matter to Him whether male or female, because He is looking at the Christ in us. Paul was urging the Galatians to see each other in this same way. The Genesis 3 curse never changed God's interaction with women, and Jesus' redemption was to change our interaction with each other.

We, as ambassadors of Heaven, as those seated in heavenly places, are to bring Heaven's reality into this world. One aspect of bringing that reality into this realm is bringing equality back to our sisters, mothers, daughters, and wives.

Name Recognition

Before we look at some of the amazing women of God who were listed as fellow ministers alongside the apostle Paul, we need to understand the power of name recognition. Author Bob Sorge gives incredible insight into this topic.

> The desire for the praise and approval of man runs very deep in our sinful flesh. We can crucify the desire for man's praise, but it keeps resurfacing in our flesh in all kinds of creative and fresh ways.
>
> Paul was aware of the insidious trap that young men fall into, for they can easily convince themselves that their motives are totally pure in seeking the praise of God alone, when in fact this desire for the praise of man is still a very strong issue within them. Paul showed his sensitivity to this issue in the way he related to one brother in the book of Second Corinthians.
>
> Here the context of the matter to which I refer:
>
> *I thank God, who put into the heart of Titus the same concern I have for you. For Titus not only welcomed our appeal, but he is*

*coming to you with much enthusiasm and on his own initiative. And we are sending along with him **the brother** who is praised by all the churches for his service to the gospel. What is more, he was chosen by the churches to accompany us as we carry the offering, which we administer in order to honor the Lord himself and to show our eagerness to help. We want to avoid any criticism of the way we administer this liberal gift. For we are taking pains to do what is right, not only in the eyes of the Lord but also in the eyes of men.*

*In addition, we are sending with them **our brother** who has often proved to us in many ways that he is zealous, and now even more so because of his great confidence in you. As for Titus, he is my partner and fellow worker among you; as for our brothers, they are representatives of the churches and an honor to Christ* (2 Corinthians 8:16-23).

Paul is writing about two brothers—Titus and an unnamed brother. Titus is mentioned twice by name and commended; the other brother is left nameless. Why does Paul not mention the other brother's name? Because Paul knew the power of name recognition.

There's something intoxicating about seeing your name in print and having your name known by others. I've tasted of that wine personally just a little bit; Paul also knew all about that. And he was aware that the brother to whom he was referring didn't have the maturity to handle the fame properly. So Paul refused to make his name known. There's no doubt in my mind that the unnamed brother was young, new in ministry, and still in training. Titus, on the other hand, was safe to name because of his evident maturity and proven faithfulness.

We might think this was an accidental oversight on Paul's part until we realize that he repeated the same thing the second time in the same epistle. The following verse comes four chapters later:

*I urged Titus to go to you and I sent **our brother** with him. Titus did not exploit you, did he? Did we not act in the same spirit and follow the same course?* (2 Corinthians 12:18)

For the second time, Paul mentions Titus twice by name while leaving his companion nameless.[2]

Considering this profound insight about name recognition, let us apply this to the topic of women in leadership. Keep in mind that the apostle Paul, who avoided mentioning the name of Titus's traveling companion, did not hesitate to commend many female ministers in his writings.

PAUL'S CO-LABORERS

In Romans chapter 16, Paul points out many women by name without hesitation. This speaks volumes about the level of their character and leadership in the early Church. For example, the chapter starts by acknowledging a female deacon named Phoebe.

*I commend to you our sister **Phoebe, a deaconess** of the church in Cenchrea. I ask you to receive her in the Lord in a way worthy of the saints and to give her any help she may need from you, for she has been a great help to many people, including me* (Romans 16:1-2).

Then Paul acknowledges Priscilla and Aquila in verses 3 and 4. Look closely, and you will see that he makes a statement that wouldn't even be proper in modern times. Paul put the wife's name first. Even in modern etiquette this is considered taboo. Etiquette states that we address a couple as Mr. and Mrs. Jonathan and Karen Welton. It would be considered improper and poor taste to address a couple as Karen and Jonathan Welton. Yet, the apostle has no qualms about acknowledging Pricilla first and her husband second.

> *Greet* **Priscilla** *and Aquila, my fellow workers in Christ Jesus. They risked their lives for me. Not only I but all the churches of the Gentiles are grateful to them* (Romans 16:3-4).

Paul continues and acknowledges Mary, Tryphena, Tryphosa, and Persis.

> [Mary served in ministry:] *Greet* **Mary**, *who worked very hard for you* (Romans 16:6).

> *Greet* **Tryphena and Tryphosa**, *those women who work hard in the Lord. Greet my dear friend* **Persis**, *another woman who has worked very hard in the Lord* (Romans 16:12).

Considering the caution that Paul used regarding name recognition, it is a powerful statement that he named so many female co-workers in Romans 16. It is unfortunate that Paul has been given such a bad reputation of supposedly suppressing women. I believe that much of the Church has misunderstood much of what Paul actually wrote regarding women. I will show you later in this chapter how some of these misunderstandings have occurred.

FEMALE APOSTLES AND PROPHETS

By examining Romans 16, we can see that Paul was very much in favor of women in ministry, but as yet, we have not seen high positions of authority given to women in Scripture, so let's continue our investigation.

*And in the church God has appointed **first of all apostles, second prophets**, third teachers, then workers of miracles, also those having gifts of healing, those able to help others, those with gifts of administration, and those speaking in different kinds of tongues* (1 Corinthians 12:28).

We understand from this passage that apostles are the highest position of authority in the Church. In fact, Ephesians 2:20 tells us that the apostles and prophets are the foundation of the Church. Therefore, if a woman could be an apostle or a prophet, wouldn't it stand to reason that she could be placed in lower positions of authority such as evangelist, teacher, or pastor? I would believe that stands to reason!

There are four women listed as prophetesses in the Bible, three in the Old Testament and one in the New Testament. (Note: The title *prophetess* has no less authority than the male equivalent of *prophet*, because they come from the same root word.)

The first is Miriam:

Then Miriam the prophetess, Aaron's sister, took a tambourine in her hand, and all the women followed her, with tambourines and dancing (Exodus 15:20).

The second is Deborah, who was not only a prophetess, but was the leader of Israel:

Deborah, a prophetess, the wife of Lappidoth, was leading Israel at that time (Judges 4:4).

The third is Huldah the prophetess:

Hilkiah the priest…went to speak to the prophetess Huldah… (2 Kings 22:14).

The fourth is our New Testament example, Anna:

There was also a prophetess, Anna, the daughter of Phanuel, of the tribe of Asher. She was very old; she had lived with her husband seven years after her marriage (Luke 2:36).

From these four examples we can see that God has no problem having a woman as a prophet, the second highest level of authority in the Church. If a woman can be a prophet, then she can be a lower position, like a senior pastor, right? But what about an apostle? Is there any evidence of a female apostle in the New Testament?

Yes! There is a clear example of a female apostle in the New Testament. In fact she and her husband are both listed together as apostles, and not just ordinary apostles, but they are called *"outstanding among the apostles."*

*Greet Andronicus and **Junias**, my relatives who have been in prison with me. They are outstanding among the apostles, and they were in Christ before I was* (Romans 16:7).

There is no scholarly rebuttal to the fact that Junias was a first century female name. Interestingly, the name Junias, is a derivative of the name Juno, the Roman goddess and wife of Jupiter. As the patroness of marriage, Juno was sought after for the dilation of the cervix for safe child delivery. Junias was without question a female name, so this passage of Scripture is proof of a female apostle.

Average Christianity argues over what position a woman can hold in ministry. Some will allow a woman to teach children, some will let her teach the youth group, some will say she can hold administrative roles, and sometimes maybe she can be an assistant pastor, but typically the role of senior pastor is out of the question.

The concept that a female cannot be in the sacred position of senior pastor is biblically hard to defend. When the word *pastor* is examined in Scripture, there is a major flaw in the argument. If you were to look up the word *pastor* in a concordance, you would find that it is only used once in all of the New Testament (see Eph. 4:11). Even in this one reference, there is no definition or instruction as to who can and cannot be a pastor. Yet culturally we have created definitions that restrict women from access to the most vague of all New Testament leadership gifts.

We have seen that women can reside in the highest places of authority in the Church as apostles and prophets. Therefore, they rightfully can hold any of the lower gifts or callings throughout the Church. However, many churches have banned women from these positions because of three passages in the New Testament. Let us investigate these highly debated verses.

THE TROUBLE VERSES

Case #1: First Peter 3:6-7

The late Bible teacher, Kenneth E. Hagin has a great insight into this verse and its application. Here is what he has to say about First Peter 3:6-7:

> Peter cites Sarah as a model wife whose worthy example Christian wives could follow.
>
> *They were **submissive** to their own husbands, like Sarah, who **obeyed** Abraham and called him her master. You are her daughters if you do what is right and do not give way to fear* (1 Peter 3:5-6).
>
> It is possible to lift this one verse out and say, *"See, the wife is to obey her husband just as Sarah obeyed Abraham."* But does it mean the wife doesn't have any right to speak her own mind? Some would leave the impression the wife never has a right to express her thoughts, that she's under the rule—the obedience—the domination—and is nothing more than a slave. But that isn't what Peter is saying. Let's see what the law says:

*Then Sarai said to Abram, "You are responsible for the wrong I
am suffering. I put my servant in your arms, and now that she
knows she is pregnant, she despises me. May the LORD judge
between you and me." "Your servant is in your hands," Abram
said. "Do with her whatever you think best." Then Sarai mis-
treated Hagar; so she fled from her* (Genesis 16:5, 6).

Here we see Abram letting Sarai have her own way. He isn't
dominating her like some warlord. From the 16th chapter
of Genesis through the 21st there is an account of a disagreement. At its climax, we see that Abraham gave in to his
wife's contention, and let her have her own way. And we see
that God justified not him, but her."

*"And she said to Abraham, "Get rid of that slave woman and her
son, for that slave woman's son will never share in the inheri-
tance with my son Isaac." The matter distressed Abraham greatly
because it concerned his son. But God said to him, "Do not be so
distressed about the boy and your maidservant. Listen to whatever Sarah tells you, because it is through Isaac that your off-
spring will be reckoned"* (Genesis 21:10-12).

God told Abraham, one time at least, to listen to his wife.
According to this, Sarah ruled her husband on this occasion.
And God approved of it, as He always does when a wife is
right."[3]

There has also been a tendency in the Church to view women as unquali-
fied for places of high leadership because they are considered the "weaker
vessel." This comes from a misapplication of First Peter 3:7.

*Husbands, in the same way be considerate as you live with
your wives, and treat them with respect as the weaker partner*

[weaker vessel (KJV)] *and as heirs with you of the gracious gift of life, so that nothing will hinder your prayers* (1 Peter 3:7).

First of all, Peter is speaking about the husband and wife relationship. Notice how he starts by saying, *"Husbands."* Second, he tells the husband three things about how to treat his wife: *be considerate, with respect, as co-heirs.* He even gives an ominous warning about how the husband's prayers could be hindered if he doesn't get this right. Then he uses the phrase, *"weaker partner,"* in the middle of the passage. In this case, the King James Version brings more clarity. In the King James Version, the phrase is rendered as *"weaker vessel."* The word *vessel* refers to dishware, as in a plate or a bowl. So to say that a wife is a weaker bowl or plate is essentially to say that a wife is to be treated like *fine china.*

Fine china is not your typical dinnerware that you throw in the dishwasher and then into the cupboard. No, it requires a gentleness that carefully washes it by hand, and it is usually displayed in a glass-front china cabinet where all can admire it. *Women are fine china and should be treated with respect, gentleness, and considerateness* is the correct understanding of the phrase *"weaker vessel."*

Case #2: First Timothy 2:11-14

A woman should learn in quietness and full submission. I do not permit a woman to teach or to have authority over a man; she must be silent. For Adam was formed first, then Eve. And Adam was not the one deceived; it was the woman who was deceived and became a sinner (1 Timothy 2:11-14).

Without understanding the correct context, it is easy to see how these verses are used to oppress women. In any careful study of the letters of Paul, the first thing that must be done is answer the following questions: To whom is the letter written? What is it regarding? Is this directive applicable to every person, everywhere, for all time?

When verses of the Bible are not in proper context, it is easy for them to be misused. For example, we must understand that Paul was speaking in hyperbole and frustration when he said, *"As for those agitators, I wish they would go the whole way and emasculate themselves"* (Gal. 5:12). Yet, if we do not understand these verses in their proper context, it would be easy to create a eunuch cult. This is no exaggeration; over the years many thousands of people have participated in suicide cults based on slight misteachings of the Bible. It is desperately important that we look closely at what we believe and why.

There is an important saying, *Right teaching leads to right living*, and it would make sense that the opposite is also true, *Wrong teaching leads to wrong living*. Wrong teaching about women in leadership has led the Church to the mistreatment of women for hundreds of years.

Question #1: To whom was the letter written? First Timothy is a letter from the apostle Paul to his spiritual son Timothy, who at that point was recognized as an apostle in Ephesus. A close look at the following passages reveals the problems in Ephesus. Here is what Paul was writing to Timothy about.

> *Have nothing to do with godless myths and old wives' tales; rather, train yourself to be godly* (1 Timothy 4:7).

> *Besides, they get into the habit of being idle and going about from house to house. And not only do they become idlers, but also gossips and busybodies, saying things they ought not to* (1 Timothy 5:13).

Question #2: What is it regarding? From these verses, as well as the historical evidence, we learn that one of the major problems in the Ephesian church was women going from house to house spreading evil teachings and doctrines of demons (see 1 Tim. 4:1). We are informed in chapter 1 that the reason for writing to Timothy was to correct this issue. Some translations say to *command certain men not to teach*, but the roots of this verse show that it was a gender neutral statement, *command certain persons not to teach*. This is important because it was actually women who were teaching erroneous doctrines in Ephesus. Paul wanted them silenced, not because of gender, but because of heresy.

> *As I urged you when I went into Macedonia, stay there in Ephesus so that you may command* **certain people** *not to teach false doctrines any longer or to devote themselves to myths and endless genealogies. Such things promote controversial speculations rather than advancing God's work—which is by faith* (1 Timothy 1:3-4 NIV).

As we have seen, the issue was not certain men, but more accurately certain women. Today's New International Version has done a great job translating in this case because the nongender specific Greek pronoun *tisi* is used here.

Question #3: Is this directive applicable to every person, everywhere, for all time? This personal letter between Paul and Timothy is not broadly applicable to all churches everywhere. Some of it is personal, contextual advice. Paul had left Timothy in charge of the church in Ephesus, and Timothy had to straighten out the false teachings by the local women. We must apply the words of Paul in a little less personal and a little more contextual manner.

For example, Paul told Timothy to stir up the gift that is in him from when Paul laid hands upon him. Obviously you and I have not had the apostle Paul lay hands on us for impartation of spiritual gifts, but that does not mean that we can disregard this verse. We must treat this verse in context as something we can still learn from. We learn from this that spiritual gifts can be imparted by the laying on of hands and that they need to be stirred up within us as well. Scripture must be kept inside its correct context.

Author J. Lee Grady gives insight into the situation that Timothy was dealing with in Ephesus.

Bible scholars have documented the fact that bizarre Gnostic heresies were circulating throughout the region at that time, and these false teachings posed a serious threat to the infant Christian churches that were budding in that part of the world. That's why so much of Paul's message to Timothy deals with how to guard against false teaching.

This teaching most certainly bred unhealthy attitudes among some women in the Ephesian church. These women were completely unlearned, but they were spreading false doctrines, and in some cases they were claiming to be teachers of the law and demanding an audience. They were most likely mixing Christian and Jewish teachings with strange heresies and warped versions of Bible stories. Some even taught that Eve was created before Adam and that she "liberated" the world when she listened to the serpent.[4]

...For Adam was formed first, then Eve. And Adam was not the one deceived; it was the woman who was deceived and became a sinner (1 Timothy 2:11-14).

What Mr. Grady has written explains why Paul would write such a seemingly out of place statement—the culture at that time was saturated with false teachings about what took place in the Garden of Eden, who was created first, and who was deceived. Ephesus at the time was the seat of the fertility goddess Diana (see Acts 19), and the new believers who were getting saved out of the occult were young in the Lord and very confused by their past. Paul was teaching Timothy how to manage his situation as the leader. The direction from Paul is a very specific and unusual context, which should not be applied to everyone, everywhere, for all time.

To gain more insight into what was really going on in Ephesus, we need to look closely at the phrase *"to have authority over."* The root word used for authority in the verse is *authentein*, and it is used only one time in the New

Testament. The Greek word that is typically used for authority in the New Testament is *exousia*. *"I do not permit a woman to teach or **to have authority** over a man; she must be silent"* (1 Tim. 2:12).

Bible scholars have noted that *authentein* has a forceful and extremely negative connotation. It implies a more specific meaning than "to have authority over" and can be translated "to dominate," "to usurp," or "to take control." Often when this word was used in ancient Greek literature, it was associated with violence or even murder. A clearer picture of what Paul told Timothy is that he doesn't allow a woman to violently steal authority. But are we to think that Paul would allow a man to violently steal authority just because he is a man? Obviously, the issue was not gender. In reference to this specific problem, Paul was instructing Timothy not to allow these women who were trying to take control and usurp authority.

In Paul's letter to Titus, Paul addressed a similar problem. In this case, it was men who were causing the problem.

> *For there are many rebellious **men**, empty talkers and deceivers, especially those of the circumcision, **who must be silenced** because they are upsetting whole families, teaching things **they should not teach** for the sake of sordid gain* (Titus 1:10-11 NASB).

The fact that this verse has never been used to tell all men everywhere that they must be silent and cannot teach is indicative of the one-sided approach that the Church has taken toward women. It is time to stop taking Scripture out of context and using it to abuse women.

Case #3: First Corinthians 14:34-35

> *...As in all the congregations of the saints, women should remain silent in the churches. They are not allowed to speak, but must be in submission, as the Law says. If they want to inquire about something, they should ask their own husbands at home; for it is*

disgraceful for a woman to speak in the church (1 Corinthians 14:33-35).

In our previous trouble verse, we looked at the situational context and how the words from Paul to Timothy do not apply to everyone, everywhere for all time. Yet when we look at this last and most troubling of the three trouble verses, it seems to be the harshest.

Regarding subjugation of women, it states the following:

† This rule applies to all congregations (everyone, everywhere, for all time).

† They must be silent in church.

† They are not allowed to speak.

† No asking questions.

† It is disgraceful for a woman to speak in church.

The first thing that must be understood about First Corinthians is that it is a response letter to the Corinthians. They wrote to Paul, and he is writing back, *"Now for the matters you wrote about..."* (1 Cor. 7:1). This puts the situation into context.

As one would with any response letter, Paul at times quotes from the Corinthians original letter to put his response into context. We are not able to see this in our modern English versions, but by looking closely at the original Greek, we can see that certain parts of First Corinthians were not written by Paul, but were quotes from their first letter to him. This is key to explaining First Corinthians 14:33-35.

It is visible in the Greek that First Corinthians 14:33-35 is a quote from the original letter to Paul. If Paul taught that it is disgraceful for a woman to even speak in church, then why would he spend time teaching that women should have their heads covered when prophesying in church (see 1 Cor. 11:2-16)? Prophesying is more than speaking; it is speaking *for* God, so if it is a shame for a woman to speak, wouldn't it be worse to claim that she is speaking for God?

If we step back from just focusing on First Corinthians 14:33-35 and look at the verses before and after, we will see the dialogue that is taking place between Paul and the Corinthians.

What then shall we say, brothers? When you come together, **everyone** *has a hymn, or a word of instruction, a revelation, a tongue or an interpretation. All of these must be done for the strengthening of the church. If anyone speaks in a tongue, two— or at the most three—should speak, one at a time, and someone must interpret. If there is no interpreter, the speaker should keep quiet in the church and speak to himself and God.*

Two or three prophets should speak, and the others should weigh carefully what is said. And if a revelation comes to someone who is sitting down, the first speaker should stop. For **you can all prophesy** *in turn so that* **everyone** *may be instructed and encouraged. The spirits of prophets are subject to the control of prophets.* **For God is not a God of disorder but of peace** (1 Corinthians 14:26-33).

As in all the congregations of the saints, women should remain silent in the churches. They are not allowed to speak, but must be in submission, as the Law says. If they want to inquire about something, they should ask their own husbands at home; for it is disgraceful for a woman to speak in the church (1 Corinthians 14:33-35). [This is the quoted portion.]

Did the word of God originate with you? Or are you the only people it has reached? If anybody thinks he is a prophet or spiritually gifted, let him acknowledge that what I am writing to you is the Lord's command. If he ignores this, he himself will be ignored. Therefore, my brothers, be eager to prophesy, and do not forbid speaking in tongues. **But everything should be done in a fitting and orderly way** (1 Corinthians 14:36-40).

In verses 26-33, Paul is teaching how a church service should be so that everyone can participate; then in verses 33-35, he quotes from the Corinthian's letter to him regarding their philosophy of how to run a service. Paul immediately responds in verses 36-40 with a very harsh rebuke to the Corinthian leaders. Apparently he strongly disagreed with their thoughts expressed in verses 33-35.

There is a sensible flow to Paul's response when we see the quoted section in the middle. Paul even uses the same language in both of his statements, *"For God is not a God of disorder but of peace...everything should be done in a fitting and orderly way"* (1 Cor. 14:33,40). And of course, Paul is not contradicting what he said earlier about how a woman should prophesy in church.

With these common misunderstandings in the previous three passages, it is easy to understand how many Christian leaders have oppressed women from leadership. Please understand that most Christian leaders are just trying to follow the Word to the best of their understanding. If they have not been shown the errors in these teachings, then they are taking these verses at face value and trying to be obedient without malicious intention.

CONCLUSION

For hundreds of years, women have been oppressed and suppressed by male chauvinistic Church leadership. The terrible misconception is that the Bible is sexist. Unfortunately, when the Bible is read with only a surface understanding, it appears to say some negative things about women. The reality is that the Bible strongly speaks of freedom and equality between the genders. I am hopeful that through reading this chapter and taking a closer look together, many lives will have new freedom, deeper healing, and restoration between genders.

ACTIVATION: FOR WOMEN

Consider each of the times that male leadership has suppressed or oppressed you from taking a place of leadership that God had called you to. Now go through each one of those memories and release forgiveness in the same manner that we did at the end of the Clean Conscience chapter.

ACTIVATION: FOR MEN

Ask the Holy Spirit to convict you of any times that you may have suppressed a woman from leadership based solely on gender. If any times come to mind, first repent to the Lord for your sin, and then ask the Lord to lead you in how to make restitution. Perhaps you need to meet with the individual face-to-face to apologize, or perhaps over the phone or through a letter. As the Lord leads you, correct your previous error and the harm that it caused.

ACKNOWLEDGMENTS

To my friends Gretchen Humphrey and Debra Hogervorst. If I could clone each of you a thousand times and put you in leadership positions all over the Body of Christ, I would. You two are some of my favorite female leaders; I am so proud to know you and be known by you. Thank you for your friendship with Karen and me; we trust you with our lives and our hearts.

ENDNOTES

1. Richard T. Ritenbaugh, *Forerunner Commentary*, http://bibletools. org/index.cfm/fuseaction/Bible.show/bibleBook/1/sChap/3/ sVerse/3/sVerseID/72/eVerseID/72/opt/comm/RTD/cgg/ version/kjv; accessed February 11, 2011.

2. Bob Sorge, *Dealing with the Rejection and Praise of Man* (Lee's Summit, MO: Oasis House, 1999), 39-40.

3. Kenneth E. Hagin, *The Woman Question* (Tulsa, OK: Rhema Bible Church, 1983), 16-17.

4. J. Lee Grady, *10 Lies the Church Tells Women: How the Bible has been misused to keep women in spiritual bondage* (Lake Mary, FL: Charisma House, 2000), 57.

CHAPTER EIGHT

BUILDING THE
DIVINE OTTOMAN

...For the darkness is disappearing and the true light
is already shining (1 John 2:8b NLT).

BELL LABS ANNOUNCE "DARK SUCKER THEORY"

For years it has been believed that electric bulbs emitted light. However, recent information from Bell Labs has proven otherwise. Electric bulbs don't emit light; they suck dark. Thus they now call these bulbs dark suckers. The dark sucker theory, according to a spokesman from the Labs, proves the existence of dark, that dark has mass heavier than that of light, and that dark is faster than light.

The basis of the dark sucker theory is that electric bulbs suck dark. Take for example the dark suckers in the room where you are. There is less dark right next to them than there is elsewhere. The larger the dark sucker, the greater its capacity to suck dark. Dark suckers in a parking lot have a much greater capacity than the ones in this room.

As with all things, dark suckers don't last forever. Once they are full of dark, they can no longer suck. This is proven by the black spot on a full dark sucker. A new candle has a white wick. You will notice that after the first use, the wick turns black, representing all the dark which has been sucked into it. If you hold a pencil next to the wick of an operating candle, the tip will turn black because it got in the path of the dark flowing into the candle. Unfortunately, these primitive dark suckers have a very limited range.

There are also portable dark suckers. The bulbs in these can't handle all of the dark by themselves, and must be aided by a dark storage unit. When the dark storage unit is full, it must be either emptied or replaced before the portable dark sucker can operate again.

Dark has mass. When dark goes into a dark sucker, friction from this mass generates heat. Thus it is not wise to touch an operating dark sucker. Candles present a special problem, as the dark must travel in the solid wick instead of through glass. This generates a great amount of heat. Thus it can be very dangerous to touch an operating candle.

Dark is also heavier than light. If you swim deeper and deeper, you notice it gets darker and darker. When you reach a depth of approximately fifty feet, you are in total darkness. This is because the heavier dark sinks to the bottom of the lake and the lighter light floats to the top.

The immense power of dark can be utilized to a man's advantage. We can collect the dark that has settled to the bottom of lakes and push it through turbines, which generates electricity and helps push it to the ocean where it may be safely stored. Prior to turbines, it was much more difficult to get dark from rivers and lakes to the ocean. The Indians recognized this problem and tried to solve it. When on a river in a canoe traveling in the same direction as the flow of dark, they paddled slowly, so as not to stop the flow of dark, but when they traveled against the flow of dark, they paddled quickly so as to help push the dark along its way.

Finally, we must prove that dark is faster than light. If you stand in an illuminated room in front of a closed, dark closet, then slowly open the door, you would see the light slowly enter the closet, but since the dark is so fast, you would not be able to see the dark leave the closet.

In conclusion, Bell Labs stated that dark suckers make all our lives much easier. So the next time you look at an electric light bulb, remember that it is indeed a dark sucker.[1]

This fictional news report shows how laughable it is when there is ignorance regarding the true nature of light and darkness. Unfortunately, the Average Christian has been taught certain concepts about light and darkness that are no laughing matter. These concepts are disempowering and crippling the Body of Christ from rising up and living as Normal Christians.

Many Average Christians have been taught that the light of God's people and the darkness of satan's kingdom will both increase simultaneously. This teaching developed from what I believe to be a misunderstanding of Isaiah 60. Read the following passage and take a moment to determine if you think it is saying that light and darkness grow simultaneously.

Arise, shine, for your light has come, and the glory of the Lord rises upon you. See, darkness covers the earth and thick darkness is over the peoples, but the Lord rises upon you and His glory appears over you. Nations will come to your light, and kings to the brightness of your dawn (Isaiah 60:1-3).

I can understand from where the confusion has come. It would seem from a surface reading that Isaiah was observing darkness and light together as parallels. Yet upon closer inspection, we find that Isaiah was not observing them together. Look again at verse 1. *"Arise, shine, for your light has come, and the glory of the LORD rises upon you"* (Isa. 60:1). Notice the verb tense, *"Arise, shine."* These are commands telling someone who is currently not standing to arise, spoken in the future tense. *Arise and shine* is something that the hearer is commanded to do in the momentary future.

The next verse is a comment on the current state of affairs and speaks to the present tense. *"See, darkness covers the earth and thick darkness is over the peoples..."* (Isa. 60:2a). Notice the word *see,* which would mean to look around or observe in the present. Picture with me that Isaiah was perhaps in a vision. In this vision he *sees* that in the present *darkness covers the earth and thick darkness is over the peoples.* Then he hears the voice of the Holy Spirit declare, *Arise! Shine! For your light has come and the glory of the Lord rises upon you!* Because of the order of these two sentences, we have overlooked that the verb tenses actually reverse their order. By putting verse 2 before verse 1, we receive much clarity.

To paraphrase these verses in chronological order, it would go something like this, "Hey Isaiah, look around yourself and notice all the darkness. Now look over there and see the light that is rising from the glory of the Lord. Soon My glory will dispel the darkness and the nations will come to My light."

WHAT WAS ISAIAH SEEING?

Another problem that has come from this passage is the interpretation of the phrase, *darkness covers the earth and thick darkness is over the peoples.* Throughout history "doom-and-gloom prophets" have been declaring that the end is near because of how thick the spiritual darkness is. Yet perhaps

Isaiah was not even talking about *spiritual* or *metaphorical* darkness. What if he was prophetically seeing a time of physical darkness? If so, was there a time in history when darkness covered the whole earth? If we can find an answer to that question, we can find the time that Isaiah was seeing. I suggest that Isaiah was actually seeing and prophesying about the following event.

> *It was now about the sixth hour, and darkness came over the whole land until the ninth hour, for the sun stopped shining. And the curtain of the temple was torn in two* (Luke 23:44-45).

The Jewish day starts at 6 A.M. Thus, the sixth hour would be 12 noon, and the ninth hour would be 3 P.M. This means that the sun stopped shining from noon until 3 P.M., the brightest three hours of the day, especially bright in the desert climate of Israel. I would like you to consider that Isaiah was prophetically seeing a specific day when literal darkness covered the earth (see Luke 23), and then he saw God speaking to His people saying, *"Arise, shine, for your light has come, and the glory of the LORD rises upon you"* (Isa. 60:1). And when did this glory of the Lord come upon His people? I believe that the day of Pentecost fits the description perfectly.

> *When the day of Pentecost came, they were all together in one place. Suddenly a sound like the blowing of a violent wind came from heaven and filled the whole house where they were sitting. They saw what seemed to be tongues of fire that separated and came to rest on each of them. All of them were filled with the Holy Spirit and began to speak in other tongues as the Spirit enabled them* (Acts 2:1-4).

This fulfills Isaiah 60:3-5, which speaks of how once the glory had risen upon His people, the nations would turn to the light.

> *Nations will come to your light, and kings to the brightness of your dawn. Lift up your eyes and look about you: All assemble*

and come to you; your sons come from afar, and your daughters are carried on the arm. Then you will look and be radiant, your heart will throb and swell with joy; the wealth on the seas will be brought to you, to you the riches of the nations will come (Isaiah 60:3-5).

This is why Jesus instructed His disciples to *"...make disciples of all nations..."* (Matt. 28:19). He knew that Luke 23 would fulfill the prophecy of darkness that Isaiah saw and that the day of Pentecost would release the glory of the Lord as Isaiah had prophesied. Soon the disciples would see Isaiah 60:3-5, where the nations turn toward the light, take place. Therefore, they needed to be ready to disciple those nations.

The Advancing Kingdom

If you are willing to reconsider your understanding of Isaiah 60 in light of what I am sharing, then you will probably have to consider shifting your perspective on the Kingdom of Light versus the kingdom of darkness. For one, I am not waiting for the world to get darker and darker before the light arises. The world literally went dark on the day of Jesus' crucifixion, and Isaiah spoke of it prophetically. Since the day of Pentecost, we have been experiencing the glory of God arising and taking back planet Earth from the powers of satan, sin, and death. We are currently overcoming evil with good everywhere the Kingdom of God spreads. *"Do not be overcome by evil, but overcome evil with good"* (Rom. 12:21).

In eighth grade Earth Science class, I was taught that it is impossible for light and dark to grow simultaneously. Yet somehow this is being taught from pulpits regularly. A preacher will speak of how dark the impending doom is over a generation or region and then will try to balance these comments by saying that the glory of the Lord will rise and that it will simultaneously be darker and lighter. This is impossible in every conceivable way.

To demonstrate the error involved in this type of thinking, imagine a lamp containing a three-way light bulb. The lamp is at 50 watts. As you turn the lamp to 100 watts consider, *Where in the room did it just get darker?* Now turn the lamp to 150 watts and repeat the question, *Where in the room did it just get darker?* Of course it did not get darker anywhere in the room because you turned up the light. There is no tension between light and dark. They are incompatible. They do not cohabitate; light displaces darkness.

Light aggressively takes ground away from darkness. The very nature of the Kingdom of Light is that it is always advancing and progressing. Take for example the following five progressive statements from Scripture. The Word says that we move from:

Brighter to brighter:

The path of the righteous is like the first gleam of dawn, shining ever brighter till the full light of day (Proverbs 4:18).

Grace to grace:

And of His fullness we have all received, and grace for grace (John 1:16 NKJV).

Strength to strength:

They go from strength to strength... (Psalm 84:7 NKJV).

Faith to faith:

For in it the righteousness of God is revealed from faith to faith; as it is written, "The just shall live by faith" (Romans 1:17 NKJV).

Glory to glory:

But we all, with unveiled face, beholding as in a mirror the glory of the Lord, are being transformed into the same image from glory to glory, just as by the Spirit of the Lord (2 Corinthians 3:18 NKJV).

According to these verses, it would be accurate to say that the Church is currently walking in the greatest brightness, grace, strength, faith, and glory that it ever has. This is very hard for some to accept, but it is true. Jesus set in motion a Kingdom that is still progressing and being established more and more each day. *"Of the increase of His government and peace there shall be no end..."* (Isa. 9:7 NKJV). It will continue to progress until it has fulfilled the following verses:

...For the earth will be filled with the knowledge of the LORD as the waters cover the sea (Isaiah 11:9 NKJV).

For the earth will be filled with the knowledge of the glory of the LORD, as the waters cover the sea (Habakkuk 2:14 NKJV).

But truly, as I live, all the earth shall be filled with the glory of the LORD (Numbers 14:21 NKJV).

Many have a hard time believing that the Church is doing so well because they do not have a global perspective. Unfortunately, the Average Christian is informed more by CNN and end-time novels than by what the Word actually says. But according to the facts and the Lord's Word, we are winning and will continue to do so until every enemy of Christ has been made His footstool.

When the Lord Jesus had finished talking with them, He was taken up into heaven and sat down at God's right hand (Mark 16:19 TLB).

But when this Priest had offered for all time one sacrifice for sins, He sat down at the right hand of God. Since that time He waits for His enemies to be made His footstool (Hebrews 10:12-13).

Then the end will come, when He hands over the kingdom to God the Father after He has destroyed all dominion, authority and power. For He must reign until He has put all His enemies under His feet. The last enemy to be destroyed is death (1 Corinthians 15:24-26).

Jesus has been sitting at the right hand of God for 2,000 years waiting while His Church builds Him a Divine Ottoman of sorts. The assignment of the Church for the last 2,000 years has been to crush satan under our feet—*"The God of peace will soon crush Satan under your feet"* (Rom. 16:20a)—and thus put Jesus' enemies under His feet. As delegated authorities, by crushing satan under our feet, we are placing satan under Jesus' feet.

Jesus said that His Kingdom is one of continual growth. "The Kingdom of Heaven is like a mustard seed planted in a field. It is the smallest of all seeds, but it becomes the largest of garden plants; it grows into a tree, and birds come and make nests in its branches" (see Matt. 13:31-32). "The Kingdom of Heaven is like the yeast a woman used in making bread. Even though she put only a little yeast in three measures of flour, it permeated every part of the dough" (see Matt. 13:33).

A final thought on God's ever advancing Kingdom is found in Ezekiel 47:1-5. Ezekiel had a prophetic experience with the river of God. He waded into the water and took four measurements. The first measurement had the water at ankle level, the second at the knees, the third up to the waist, and the final measurement had the water over his head. This is a clear picture of the nature of the Kingdom of God; it is always progressing, becoming deeper and wider, and covering more ground. That is what has been happening for 2,000 years while Average Christians are sitting around waiting to lose to the devil. Yet, Normal Christians are aligned with King Jesus and busy co-laboring in the takeover of this planet.

HISTORICAL PERSPECTIVE

Many Average Christians have no optimistic view of the future because they have a lack of perspective regarding the past. When they look back, they think that they are seeing the good ol' days. However, with a better grasp on history, we will see that God has been steadily progressing His Kingdom forward.

To see this improvement, let's lift ourselves to a higher perspective from which we can look over the course of history. We know what life is like today, but let's compare it to the conditions of society in the past. (The following comes from the prolific author, Harold Eberle.)

Start by taking a snapshot of what life was like in the United States 200 years ago. In the early 1800s there were about 5 million people who had immigrated or were descendants of immigrants, but 20 percent of them were slaves. The age of sexual consent in many states was 9 or 10 years old. Abortion was legal throughout most of the 19th century, and records tell us that over one fifth of all pregnancies were aborted, with Michigan having the highest rate at 34 percent. Prostitution in New York City was commonplace with approximately one prostitute for every 64 men; the mayor of Savannah estimated that his city had one for every 39.

Thousands of people were moving West and many had no formal church buildings to attend until years after they had settled and communities had been developed. Tens of thousands of Native Americans were being murdered or forced off their lands. Thousands of Chinese people were being brought in to serve as forced laborers. When gold was discovered in various regions of the West, gold rushes occurred, which produced vile and dangerous communities. Many people in the West carried guns for protection because murder was commonplace. Throughout the United States women could not vote and men could legally beat their wives so long as they did not maim or kill them. Alcoholism was at a much higher incidence than it is today. Things in the United States were not better morally, ethically, or spiritually.

Of course, there were some godly individuals laying the foundations of the U.S. government, but the moral and ethical climate of America was much worse than it is today. The good ol' days were not so good.

Let's go back even further in time to take a snapshot of the whole world 2,000 years ago when Jesus was a child. The Roman Empire dominated civilization and centered on Europe, the Middle East, and Northern Africa. In Italy, approximately 40 percent of the population consisted of slaves. Throughout the Empire, homosexuality was commonplace, especially between masters and slaves. Infanticide was usually practiced on the deformed and weak; sometimes it was practiced for no other reason than the child being female. Most of the Roman and Greek people worshiped many gods such as Jupiter, Juno, and Neptune. Human beings were routinely tortured to death or mauled by wild animals in the Roman arenas. The greatest thinkers of the times thought there was nothing wrong with these practices. Ernest Hampden Cook wrote in his book *The Christ Has Come:*

> The fact is that bad as the world still is, yet morally it is vastly better than it was when Jesus was born in Bethlehem of Judea....Few people in these days have an adequate conception of the misery and degradation which were then the common lot of almost all mankind, owing the monstrous wickedness of the times, to continual wars, to the cruelties of political despotism, and of everywhere-prevailing slavery.

> Outside of the Roman Empire, people in Africa, Asia, and Australia worshiped nature, demons, and their own dead ancestors. Here in North America, tribes had many forms of worship, but no one had a revelation of the Messiah. In

South America, millions worshiped a bloodthirsty god who demanded tens of thousands of human sacrifices.

When Jesus came to the earth, there was only one tiny nation located in the Middle East that had a revelation of the one true God, and even the citizens were living in a time of great doubt. All of the rest of the world was lost in darkness. As the apostle Paul wrote:

...formerly you, the Gentiles...were at that time separated from Christ...having no hope and without God in the world (Ephesians 2:11-12).

That was the condition of the world 2,000 years ago.

Now think of how blessed the world is today. The gospel is being preached in every corner of the earth. Christianity is exploding in growth across the world, with more than 200,000 people becoming born-again Christians every day. In China there are more than 20,000 per day becoming Christians and in South America there are 35,000 per day. In total there are more than a million people per work week becoming Christians.

The tiny seed that came into the earth in that little nation of Israel has grown to permeate the earth. Christianity is, in fact, the largest, most influential force of humanity in the world today.

Still, we should not envision a utopia around the corner. Until Jesus returns there will be a struggle between righteousness and unrighteousness. There may be many difficult times ahead, and under conditions of war, hunger, disease, and lack, people can sink into beast like levels. Recognizing that human nature is frail and subject to many defects, we must not embrace a Pollyannaish view of our future.

Yet, we can be assured that the world is getting better morally, ethically, and spiritually. Of course, Christians must stay vigilant, and we have much work ahead of us, but we must not lose sight of the fact that we are gaining ground. The Kingdom of God is advancing and Jesus Christ is Lord. From this we can conclude that the Christian worldview should be a realistic, optimistic worldview.[2]

Have you been stretched by what you have just read? You may even need to read it a few more times to grasp the shift in thinking required of you. But when you are ready to be stretched some more, the following quote from author James Rutz will take you even further:

Status Update

The growing core of Christianity crosses theological lines and includes 707 million born-again people who are increasing by 8% a year. These "core apostolic" are a powerful mix of Charismatics, Pentecostals, and Evangelicals whose main distinction is that they are in expanding, connected, easily countable networks.

The term excludes those groups that are so liberal in theology, so isolated in structure, or so deeply rooted in medieval tradition that they are hardly growing at all.

We rely on God, not statistical trends. Yet it's fascinating to realize that the current core apostolic growth rate would produce a world composed entirely of apostolic Christians by 2032!

Of course, straight-line projections are a fool's game because life never goes in a straight line. There will be pockets of resistance and unforeseen breakthroughs. Still, at the rate we're growing now, to be comically precise, there would be more Christians than people by the autumn of 2032, about 8.2 billion.

In any case, the new realities are massive in scope. The future of your world is being written at this very hour. For instance:

† Up until 1960, Western Evangelicals outnumbered non-Western Evangelicals—mostly Latinos, blacks, and Asians—by two to one. As of 2000, non-Westerners had shot ahead by four to one. By 2010, it will be seven to one! (Park this in the back of your brain for the next time you hear someone bad-mouth Christianity as "the white man's religion.")

† If you go through Latin America on a Sunday morning, you will now find more evangelicals than Catholics in church.

† As soon as we produce some church models that are culturally acceptable to Hindus, we could see an additional 70 to 100 million secret Indian Christians go public.

† There are now more missionaries sent from non-Western nations than Western nations.

Are you starting to see the outline of the new world? God writes history, but human eyes have trouble reading his handwriting. It's not that he writes too small, but too big.

Every 25 Minutes

When I was a kid in Sunday school, I was really impressed that 3,000 people were saved on the day of Pentecost. I thought, Wow, that'll never happen again!

How wrong I was. It now happens around the globe every 25 minutes.

That adds up fast. Be very encouraged: By tomorrow, there will be 175,000 more Christians than there are today. That means, no matter how rotten a day you have today, no matter how many things go haywire, when the sun comes up tomorrow you will have 175,00 new brothers and sisters in Christ in 238 nations around the world!

One example of how these numbers can happen today: In Lagos, Nigeria, in November, 2000, Reinhard Bonnke held the largest crusade in world history. During the six days and nights, almost six million people came, and 3,400,000 registered decisions for Christ—1,093,745 of them on the last night!

An integral part of the Spirit's move: Hundreds of thousands were healed of every condition imaginable. Many of them were "checked out" by the 1,000 physicians who came nightly for that purpose.

You may ask, "Even with methodical Germans in charge, how on earth did they handle that many converts?" The answer is, they had 30,000 ushers and spent six months training 200,000 counselors!

Campus Crusades for Christ now estimates we will see a billion new converts in the next ten years. My numbers project a net growth of the body of Christ at a billion and a half. But any way you slice it, the kingdom is expanding at a heart pounding pace. I'm not being triumphalistic or arrogant here, I am just reporting the numbers. From 1970 to 2000, core apostolic doubled every nine years.

From our vantage point in North America and Europe, where church membership is going nowhere, this sounds like a cooked-up fantasy. But it is true. This is the biggest megashift in history. Can you think of any time when over a billion people eagerly changed their lives and loyalties in one generation?

Within a few years, at current rates, the character of whole nations will be transformed. Majorities will become minorities and vice versa.

As national strongholds of sin are dismantled and pits of misery cleaned up, the true purpose of God for many nations will be revealed. We are in the early stages of a total transformation of our planet.[3]

What Does the Future Hold?

Given this new, amazing, and optimistic view of the future, one might now ask: What is left, and what will happen in the future? Here are a few prophetic verses that are yet to be fulfilled.

Prophetic Verse #1

Husbands, love your wives, just as Christ also loved the church and gave Himself for her, that He might sanctify and cleanse her with the washing of water by the word, that He might present her to Himself a glorious church, not having spot or wrinkle or any such thing, but that she should be holy and without blemish (Ephesians 5:25-27 NKJV).

Jesus is not coming for a bratty preteen bride; He is waiting for His Bride to come into perfect maturity. She will not be a small child with spots of food that she has spilled on her dress, nor will she be an old haggard woman covered with wrinkles. She will not be too young or too old; Jesus will return based on the maturity of His beautiful Bride.

Prophetic Verse #2

*So Christ himself gave the apostles, the prophets, the evangelists, the pastors and teachers, to equip his people for works of service, so that the body of Christ may be built up until we all reach **unity in the faith** and in the knowledge of the Son of God and become mature, attaining to the whole measure of the fullness of Christ* (Ephesians 4:11-13).

According to Davis A. Barrett's World Christian Encyclopedia (2000 edition), there are 33,830 Christian denominations in the world today. I would say that we have not reached *"unity in the faith."* I will not guess at what unity in the faith looks like, but I believe it still is in our future.

Prophetic Verse #3

*I consider that our present sufferings are not worth comparing with the glory that will be revealed in us. The **creation waits in eager expectation for the sons of God to be revealed.** For the creation was subjected to frustration, not by its own choice, but by the will of the One who subjected it, in hope that the creation itself will be liberated from its bondage to decay and brought into the glorious freedom of the children of God* (Romans 8:18-21).

This is another verse for which I will not claim to have a simple explanation, yet I believe that the Lord is moving His Church toward its fulfillment. The sons of God must come forth in the earth before the end.

Prophetic Verse #4

The seventh angel sounded his trumpet, and there were loud voices in heaven, which said: **The kingdom of the world has become the kingdom of our Lord** *and of His Christ, and He will reign forever and ever* (Revelation 11:15).

Amen! We sure have a lot to look forward to!

CONCLUSION

I have purposely not included my stances on specific debatable questions of the end times. My goal in this chapter has been to show three specific things: 1) the past was not so great, 2) the present is not as bad as many claim, and 3) the future is going to be ever-increasingly glorious!

The end-times view of a Normal Christian is that we are part of a movement that is ever-progressing forward. We are not retreating; we are not losing; we are not simply holding the fort. *We are advancing and taking ground!*

ACTIVATION

It is time to purge your spiritual diet of anything that is laced with the poison of fear—a spiritual detoxification of sorts. This can include turning off news broadcasts, talk radio, and end times teaching on Christian television, throwing out Christian novels about the end times, and so forth. The fear and wrong perspectives that come through these avenues are poisonous to the victorious mindset of a Normal Christian.

ACKNOWLEDGMENT

I extend a thank you to my friend Harold Eberle. Your teaching and friendship have changed my life more than you understand. Thank you for fearlessly stretching the Body of Christ.

ENDNOTES

1. "Bell Labs Proves Existence of Dark Suckers," http://www. jokes2go.com/jokes/2636.html; accessed February 11, 2011.

2. Harold Eberle, *Christianity Unshackled, Are You a Truth Seeker?* (Shippensburg, PA: Destiny Image, 2009), 264-267.

3. James Rutz, *Mega Shift, Igniting Spiritual Power* (Colorado Springs, C: Empowerment Press, 2005), 25-27.

CHAPTER NINE

RAISING THE DEAD

Jesus never attended a funeral that He didn't mess up.
—Jonathan Welton

At six o'clock on an April evening in 2001, five-year-old Arjun Janki Dass died in New Delhi from an accidental electrocution. His parents took him to a medical clinic where they worked on his body for two hours—without success. The doctor charged them 5,000 rupees (about $110) and told them to call a mortician.

Instead they called Rodrick at the nearby Deliverance Church. He then called upon Savitri, one of his staff members. Savitri brought two other Christians to Arjun's home, and the five of them began praying over the dead body at about 10:00 P.M. They prayed their hearts out for six hours. Then at 4:00 A.M. the next morning, Arjun snapped back to life—no brain damage, no problems.

Today, he's a normal eight-year-old kid. I met Savitri, Arjun, and his mother, Mina, and the boy is fine except for a nasty scar behind his left ear where the wire hit. Savitri is a 60-year-old widow, a Dalit ("untouchable") from the lowly Dom caste. She spent her life as a street sweeper, which made her, in the caste system, the lowest of the low. The broom was her livelihood, and she remains today a fine, humble lady, a former Hindu turned to Christ.

As we were parting, I asked Savitri through an interpreter, "How many resurrections have you been involved with in the six years that you've been doing ministry?"

She answered quietly, "Sixteen." For a moment, my brain froze. Then I began to re-evaluate my life.

I would give you Savitri's e-mail address so you could check her out for yourself, but she doesn't have one. She can't read.[1]

Raising the Dead Is Part of Normal Christianity

When Jesus sent out His disciples, He said in one breath, *"Heal the sick, raise the dead, cleanse those who have leprosy, drive out demons. Freely you have received, freely give"* (Matt. 10:8). While hundreds of books and training conferences have focused on healing the sick and casting out demons, relatively nothing is taught about raising the dead. Even though Jesus put these miracles in the same breath, raising the dead has somehow been relegated to the outer fringes of the mission field. Raising the dead is not a fringe doctrine, but a basic belief in Normal Christianity (see Heb. 6:1-2).

To say that you believe in supernatural, instantaneous healing by the laying on of hands is a big stretch for many unbelieving believers in Average Christianity. So to say that you believe in raising the dead is like saying, "Hello, I am completely nuts, please lock me up and throw away the key."

The Bible, however, says, *"Why should any of you consider it incredible that God raises the dead?"* (Acts 26:8).

The Bible records that Elijah, Elisha, Peter, Paul, and of course Jesus, raised the dead. Starting with the first recorded resurrection, let's examine the biblical examples of raising the dead. Elijah was the first person to raise the dead.

> *Now it happened after these things that the son of the woman who owned the house became sick. And his sickness was so serious that there was no breath left in him. So she said to Elijah, "What have I to do with you, O man of God? Have you come to me to bring my sin to remembrance, and to kill my son?" And he said to her, "Give me your son." So he took him out of her arms and carried him to the upper room where he was staying, and laid him on his own bed. Then he cried out to the LORD and said, "O LORD my God, have You also brought tragedy on the widow with whom I lodge, by killing her son?" And he stretched himself out on the child three times, and cried out to the LORD and said, "O LORD my God, I pray, let this child's soul come back to him." Then the LORD heard the voice of Elijah; and the soul of the child came back to him, and he revived. And Elijah took the child and brought him down from the upper room into the house, and gave him to his mother. And Elijah said, "See, your son lives!" Then the woman said to Elijah, "Now by this I know that you are a man of God, and that the word of the LORD in your mouth is the truth"* (1 Kings 17:17-24 NKJV).

Elijah was the spiritual father of Elisha, and we can see from Second Kings 2 that Elisha received the double portion of Elijah's anointing. As you carefully compare the two prophet's miracle ministries, you will notice that Elijah performed eight miracles and Elisha performed 15, which is almost double the anointing that was on Elijah. The interesting piece is that Elisha actually performed 16 miracles, exactly double of Elijah, but his 16th was performed after his death—more about that story coming up. Elijah set the precedent by raising from the dead the first person ever. Elisha then followed his example and raised two people from the dead. Here is the story of Elisha's first resurrection:

> But the woman conceived, and bore a son when the appointed time had come, of which Elisha had told her. So the child grew. Now it happened one day that he went out to his father, to the reapers. And he said to his father, "My head, my head!" So he said to a servant, "Carry him to his mother." When he had taken him and brought him to his mother, he sat on her knees till noon, and then died. And she went up and laid him on the bed of the man of God, shut the door upon him, and went out.
>
> Then she called to her husband, and said, "Please send me one of the young men and one of the donkeys, that I may run to the man of God and come back." So he said, "Why are you going to him today? It is neither the New Moon nor the Sabbath." And she said, "It is well." Then she saddled a donkey, and said to her servant, "Drive, and go forward; do not slacken the pace for me unless I tell you." And so she departed, and went to the man of God at Mount Carmel. So it was, when the man of God saw her afar off, that he said to his servant Gehazi, "Look, there is the Shunammite woman. Please run now to meet her, and say to her, 'Is it well with you? Is it well with your husband? Is it well with the child?'" And she answered, "It is well." Now when she came to the man of God at the hill, she caught him by the feet, but Gehazi came near to push her away. But the man of God said, "Let her alone; for her soul is in deep distress, and the LORD has hidden it from me, and has not told me." So she said, "Did I ask a son of my lord? Did I not say, 'Do not deceive me'?" Then he said to Gehazi, "Get yourself ready, and take my staff in your hand, and be on your way. If you meet anyone, do not greet him; and

if anyone greets you, do not answer him; but lay my staff on the face of the child."

*And the mother of the child said, "As the L*ORD *lives, and as your soul lives, I will not leave you." So he arose and followed her. Now Gehazi went on ahead of them, and laid the staff on the face of the child; but there was neither voice nor hearing. Therefore he went back to meet him, and told him, saying, "The child has not awakened."*

*When Elisha came into the house, there was the child, lying dead on his bed. He went in therefore, shut the door behind the two of them, and prayed to the L*ORD. *And he went up and lay on the child, and put his mouth on his mouth, his eyes on his eyes, and his hands on his hands; and he stretched himself out on the child, and the flesh of the child became warm. He returned and walked back and forth in the house, and again went up and stretched himself out on him; then the child sneezed seven times, and the child opened his eyes.*

And he called Gehazi and said, "Call this Shunammite woman." So he called her. And when she came in to him, he said, "Pick up your son." So she went in, fell at his feet, and bowed to the ground; then she picked up her son and went out (2 Kings 4:17-37 NKJV).

Elisha was walking in double the anointing of Elijah, so he did not have one resurrection, but two! In fact Elisha carried in his body twice the anointing of his mentor, so when he died, he was still carrying the anointing for a second resurrection. After his death he raised a second person from the dead.

Once while some Israelites were burying a man, suddenly they saw a band of raiders; so they threw the man's body into Elisha's tomb. When the body touched Elisha's bones, the man came to life and stood up on his feet (2 Kings 13:21).

JESUS PERFORMED THREE RESURRECTIONS

In the Old Testament, three people were raised from the dead. Jesus raised three people from the dead in His ministry, as many as Elijah and Elisha combined.

Case #1: Widow's Son From Nain

Now it happened, the day after, that He [Jesus] *went into a city called Nain; and many of His disciples went with Him, and a large crowd. And when He came near the gate of the city, behold, a dead man was being carried out, the only son of his mother; and she was a widow. And a large crowd from the city was with her. When the Lord saw her, He had compassion on her and said to her, "Do not weep." Then He came and touched the open coffin, and those who carried him stood still. And He said, "Young man, I say to you, arise." And he who was dead sat up and began to speak. And He presented him to his mother* (Luke 7:11-15 NKJV).

Case #2: Jairus' Daughter

And behold, there came a man named Jairus, and he was a ruler of the synagogue. And he fell down at Jesus' feet and begged Him to come to his house, for he had an only daughter about twelve years of age, and she was dying. But as He went, the multitudes thronged Him.... While He was still speaking, someone came from the ruler of the synagogue's house, saying to him, "Your daughter is dead. Do not trouble the Teacher." But when Jesus heard it, He answered him, saying, "Do not be afraid; only believe, and she will be made well." When He came into the house, He permitted no one to go in except Peter, James, and John, and the father and mother of the girl. Now all wept and mourned for her; but He said, "Do not weep; she is not dead, but sleeping." And they ridiculed Him, knowing that she was dead. But He put them all outside, took her by the hand and called, saying, "Little girl, arise." Then her spirit returned, and she arose immediately. And He commanded that she be given something to eat. And her parents were astonished, but He charged them to tell no one what had happened (Luke 8:41-42,49-56 NKJV).

Case #3: Lazarus

Then Jesus, again groaning in Himself, came to the tomb. It was a cave, and a stone lay against it. Jesus said, "Take away the stone." Martha, the sister of him who was dead, said to Him, "Lord, by this time there is a stench, for he has been dead four days." Jesus said to her, "Did I not say to you that if you would believe you would see the glory of God?" Then they took away the stone from the place where the dead man was lying. And Jesus lifted up His eyes and said, "Father, I thank You that You have heard Me. "And I know that You always hear Me, but because of the people who are standing by I said this, that they may believe that You sent Me." Now when He had said these things, He cried with a loud voice, "Lazarus, come forth!" And he who had died came out bound hand and foot with graveclothes, and his face was wrapped with a cloth. Jesus said to them, "Loose him, and let him go" (John 11:38-44 NKJV).

And of course, Jesus was Himself raised from the dead, which is the foundation of all of Christianity (see Rom. 10:9-10). This is recorded in all four Gospels.

EARLY CHURCH RESURRECTIONS

Jesus told His disciples that they would do greater things than He had been doing (see John 14:12), which includes the resurrections that He performed. Jesus sent His followers (us included) to *"Heal the sick, cleanse the lepers, **raise the dead**, cast out demons. Freely you have received, freely give"* (Matt. 10:8 NKJV).

In the Book of Acts we find that the early Church did resurrect the dead. It was not just Jesus or Old Testament "Super Prophets" who raised the dead. These were fishermen and tentmakers who operated by the power of the Holy Spirit and performed resurrections. In the Book of Acts, we find two (possibly three) people raised from the dead by Normal Christians.

Case #1: Tabitha

At Joppa there was a certain disciple named Tabitha, which is translated Dorcas. This woman was full of good works and charitable deeds which she did. But it happened in those days that she became sick and died. When they had washed her, they laid her in an upper room. And since Lydda was near Joppa, and the disciples had heard that Peter was there, they sent two men to him, imploring him not to delay in coming to them. Then Peter arose and went with them. When he had come, they brought him to the upper room. And all the widows stood by him weeping, showing the tunics and garments which Dorcas had made while she was with them. But Peter put them all out, and knelt down and prayed. And turning to the body he said, "Tabitha, arise."

170

And she opened her eyes, and when she saw Peter she sat up. Then he gave her his hand and lifted her up; and when he had called the saints and widows, he presented her alive. And it became known throughout all Joppa, and many believed on the Lord (Acts 9:36-42 NKJV).

Case #2: Eutychus

Now on the first day of the week, when the disciples came together to break bread, Paul, ready to depart the next day, spoke to them and continued his message until midnight. There were many lamps in the upper room where they were gathered together. And in a window sat a certain young man named Eutychus, who was sinking into a deep sleep. He was overcome by sleep; and as Paul continued speaking, he fell down from the third story and was taken up dead. But Paul went down, fell on him, and embracing him said, "Do not trouble yourselves, for his life is in him." Now when he had come up, had broken bread and eaten, and talked a long while, even till daybreak, he departed. And they brought the young man in alive, and they were not a little comforted (Acts 20:7-12 NKJV).

Case #3: Apostle Paul

Then some Jews came from Antioch and Iconium and won the crowd over. They stoned Paul and dragged him outside the city, thinking he was dead. But after the disciples had gathered around him, he got up and went back into the city. The next day he and Barnabas left for Derbe (Acts 14:19-20).

It is debatable whether Paul was completely dead and then resurrected, or perhaps he was near death and had a miraculous healing. I merely included his story for your consideration.

There are nine (possibly ten, including Paul) resurrections recorded in Scripture—three by Old Testament prophets, three by Jesus, two (possibly three) by the early Church, and the resurrection of Jesus Himself. Perhaps we should reconsider what the apostle Paul wrote, *"Why should it be thought incredible by you that God raises the dead?"* (Acts 26:8 NKJV).

The Bible confirms that raising the dead is a Christian practice that we should embrace, not fear. Even outside of the Bible, the practice of raising the dead has continued throughout Church history and even into the modern era. Let us look at a few post biblical examples.

POST-BIBLICAL RESURRECTIONS

I believe that a majority of the people who will read this book are Protestant and most likely unfamiliar with pre-Protestant history (before 1517). Yet, most Christians are familiar with historical church heroes such as Saint Augustine, Saint Patrick, Francis Xavier, and Joan of Arc, and they hardly need any introduction.

As I move chronologically through 2,000 years of history, you may notice that the more modern names are less familiar. The likes of Mel Tari, Richard Eby, Paul Yonggi Cho, and David Hogan may not be known to you or your denomination. Yet each of these testimonies have been gathered from published sources, and some have had decades to be investigated and disproven, but to no avail.

Saint Augustine, A.D. 354-430

Two weeks before Easter in Augustine's church in Hippo, North Africa, 424 A.D., a brother and sister came to Hippo both suffering from convulsive seizures. They gave a sad account of parental rejection and came each day to pray at the shrine for healing. On Easter morning before the service, the young man was in the crowded church, praying as he held on to the screen around the reliquary (a box which held the bones which were venerated as the relics of St Stephen the Martyr). Augustine was still in the vestibule prior to entering the Church when the young man fell down as dead. People near were filled with fear. But the next moment he got up and stood staring back at them, perfectly normal and cured. Three days later the same thing happened to the sister, while Augustine was preaching about St Stephen the Martyr.[2]

Saint Patrick, A.D. 389-461

Father Albert J. Hebert, has compiled over 400 resurrection stories in his book *Raised from the Dead.* Father Hebert says of Saint Patrick, the missionary to Ireland, that he "knows of no saint for whom there are claimed so many resurrection miracles during one apostolic lifetime as for St. Patrick; there were as many as 39 of these wonders. Thirty-three are mentioned in one specific report:"

For the blind and the lame, the deaf and the dumb, the palsied, the lunatic, the leprous, the epileptic, all who labored under any disease, did he in the Name of the Holy Trinity restore unto the power of their limbs and unto entire health; and in these good deeds was he daily practiced. Thirty and three dead men, some of whom had been many years buried, did this great reviver raise from the dead, as above we have more fully recorded.[3]

Joan of Arc, 1412-1431

One of the most unique saints of all time was Joan of Arc, *La Pucelle*, the Maid of Orleans. While still in her teens she courageously and successfully led French troops against the occupying English armies; she had been so directed by "voices" of St. Michael, St. Margaret, St. Catherine, and others. Like all great saints, St. Joan was a very balanced personality; allied to her fortitude and fearlessness were gentleness and pity for the suffering.

In early March, 1430 St. Joan arrived at the village of Lagny-sur-marn, in the direction of Paris. Here she learned of a woman who was greatly depressed because she had given birth to a stillborn son. Some villagers approached Joan and asked for her intercession. The mother prayed only that the child might be brought to life long enough to be baptized and so gain Heaven.

Joan went to the church where the dead child had been laid at the feet of the statue of the Blessed Mother. Young girls of the village were praying by the small corpse.

St. Joan then added her own prayers. The baby came to life and yawned three times. Baptism was hurriedly administered. Then the baby boy died again, and his beautiful spotless baptized soul went straight to Heaven.[4]

Saint Francis Xavier, 1506-1552

St. Francis Xavier is considered to have been the greatest missionary since St. Paul. He is known as the "Apostle of the Indies," and the "Apostle of Japan." In about ten short years (1541-1552) Francis did the work of a thousand individual missionaries, spreading the Catholic Faith from Goa (Portuguese territory in western India), over South India, Ceylon, Bengal, Cape Comorin, the Moluccas, Spice Islands, Malacca, and through the China Sea to Japan where he died—alone except for one companion, a Chinese youth named Antiry, on the Japanese island of Sancian, waiting for a ship to China. On his journeys St. Francis Xavier converted hundreds of thousands, and the impact of his work lasted for centuries.

…At one time, St. Francis was preaching at Coulon, near Cape Comorin in Travancore at the southern tip of India opposite Ceylon (Sri Lanka). This was a seaport, a rough town where many Christians dishonored their name. Francis, while preaching in the Portuguese church there, felt baffled and stymied by the wall of obstinacy he met in his hardhearted listeners.

Now it happened that a man had been buried in the church the day before. St. Francis stopped preaching; he prayed to God to honor the Blood and the Name of His Son and to soften the hearts of the congregation. Then he directed a few men to open the nearby grave of the man who had been buried the day before. He had prayed in tears, and now he accompanied his directions with the burning words of holy eloquence. He told the congregation how God was pleased even to raise the dead in order to convert them.

When they opened the tomb and brought out the body, it was already giving off a stench. On Francis' orders they tore apart the shroud—to find the body already beginning to putrefy. Francis expressed his desire that they should all take note of these facts. (They could hardly escape them!) Then the saint fell on his knees, made a short prayer, and commanded the dead man, in the Name of the Living God, to arise.

The man arose—alive, vigorous and in perfect health! The onlookers were filled with awe. Those who needed it fell at the saint's feet to be baptized, and a large number of people were converted because of this miracle.[5]

Smith Wigglesworth, 1860-1947

Smith Wigglesworth the plumber turned healing evangelist is widely known for having raised many people from the dead over the course of his ministry. His personal travel assistant, Albert Hibbert, reported fourteen occasions when the dead were raised during Wigglesworth's ministry. Albert said of Smith that "sometimes he would pray; but at other times he would just speak the word."

On one occasion Smith called at the home on which the family was mourning the loss of a five year old boy. Wigglesworth stood looking at the corpse in the coffin with tears running down his cheeks. Wigglesworth requested the father to leave him alone in the room. He locked the door behind the father, lifted the corpse from the coffin and stood it up in the corner. Wigglesworth rebuked death in the name of the Lord Jesus and commanded it to surrender its victim. An amazing miracle occurred and the child returned to life.[6]

Mel Tari

Mel Tari is the famous author of *Like a Mighty Wind*, which details the story of the Indonesia revival of the late 1960s and early '70s. In his book, Mel shares the following resurrection story.

In a village in the Amfoang district we were invited to a funeral where a man had been dead for two days. The family invited us to the funeral because there were many people planning to come—as a matter of fact, hundreds—and they said, "Maybe you would have a word of comfort to give to the family." So we went.

When we arrived there, there were more than a thousand people. That man had been dead for two days and was very stinky. In our tropical country, when you're dead six hours you start to decay. But after two days—oh, I tell you, you can't stand within 100 feet of him. You smelled that smell, and it was awful. In America you cannot understand that because in your funeral services they make everything very good. In Indonesia, we don't have a way to make a dead person look so nice. The people there just look terrible in two days after they have died. When we were there and sitting with the mourners, suddenly the Lord said, "Now please go and stand around that dead person, sing songs and I will raise him back from the dead."

We went and stood around this dead person. We began to sing. You know that time, the Devil said to me, "It is awful for you to sing by this stinky man. When you are 100 feet away it is bad enough. But now that you are standing near this dead person, when you open your mouth all the filth and stench comes into your mouth. It is foolish to do this."

This is true, but I must still obey the Lord. I thought, so we began to sing. But after the first song, nothing had taken place. So we started to wonder, Lord if You're going to raise him up, please do it quickly because we can't stand to stay around this stinking man. We just can't sing any more songs by this terrible smell.

Then we sang a second song, and nothing happened.

On the fifth song, nothing happened. But on the sixth song, that man began to move his toes—and the team began to get scared. We have a story in Indonesia, that sometimes when people die they wake up and hug a person by their coffin and then die again. However, we just went ahead and sang. When we sang the seventh and eighth songs, that brother woke up, looked around and smiled.

He didn't hug anybody. He just opened his mouth and said, "Jesus has brought me back to life! Brothers and sisters, I want to tell you something. First, life never ends when you die. I've been dead for two days and I've experienced it." The second thing he said was, "Hell and heaven are real. I have experienced it. The third thing I want to tell you is, if you don't find Jesus in this life you will never go to heaven. You will be condemned to hell for sure."

After he had said these things, we opened our Bibles and confirmed his testimony by the Word of God. In the next three months as our teams ministered in that area, more than 21,000 people came to know Jesus Christ as their Savior because of this wonderful miracle of resurrection.[7]

Richard Eby, 1978

Dr. Richard Eby's story of having been raised from the dead is one of the most incredible that I have found. He details the story in his book, *Caught up to Paradise*. He was resurrected after a three-story fall that smashed his skull on the cement below. He does not have memory of his death, so his wife Maybelle fills in the details.

Maybelle has told me, since my memory of that day was mercifully erased, that we were busily sorting and packing into cartons various personal effects at the Chicago home of her departed aunt and late mother. My job was to load disposables from the second and third floors, and throw the cartons to the ground below the secondary story wooden balcony. A neighbor boy would take them to the dump.

A hollow crunching sound suddenly froze Maybelle in her tracks! She had an instant flashback of a similar sickening sound from years ago in front of Marshall-Field's Department store when a girl's body had plummeted at her feet from thirteen stories up. She says that without the sickening memory she would have continued her rummaging through the closet, assuming that it was some street noise from passing traffic. Instead, she dashed to the balcony, noted the missing railing, and gazed down in horror at my bloody, muddy body beside the broken sidewalk. The termite-eaten railing lay across the body.

Her anguished scream alerted a neighbor lady who "happened" to have the ambulance phone number handy. Her housekeeper "happened" to be there that day, and phoned her church's prayer-chain.

Maybelle quickly noted the broken railing and that I had broken the cement slab upon impact. I was laying some five yards away, head-down in a pool of mud and blood, my feet hanging in thick hedge bushes beside the sidewalk. The bloody skull was exposed with the scalp torn down over each ear. The body was already grey-white and the blood had quit flowing.

She instinctively screamed in anguish and bent to check for pulse or breath. Neither. The body was stiffly contorted, and the huge pool of bloody mud around the scalped skull spelled death. Through the parted lids she noted the dilated lifeless pupils staring fixedly. For a while she stood frozen in shock; only her mind was active as it registered her plight: "God, my Dick is dead. Help me, Lord!"

Her trance was broken by the two ambulance attendants rushing past her to check the body. They returned to the vehicle for a board stretcher and in no apparent hurry lifted the body from the bushes onto the hard surface stretcher and then out to the street and into the car. Maybelle ran through the house, grabbed her purse with identification papers, and climbed in beside the body. She noted that neither paramedic seemed in a hurry as they drove away toward the nearest trauma center hospital: no need to hurry with a D.O.A. (dead on arrival) aboard, she realized.

Yet, she still believed for a miracle. "*God,*" she prayed aloud, "*get down here right now. I need you. Don't let Dick die. I need him.*" Her fists pounded wildly on the dash board to emphasize her anguish.

"Please, lady, don't ruin our car," implored the attendant as he tried to comfort her. He rechecked the body and said something to the driver. Maybelle remembers that the red lights and siren suddenly went on, and the accelerator seemed to go wide open. *"Has God answered my prayer?"* she wondered.[8]

[Note: Richard shares the following as he began to awake in the Hospital.]

As I awoke I was shocked to find myself lying spread-eagle in Intensive Care with intravenous tubing and electrical wiring stuck in me here and there. I had no idea what had happened. I tried to move and found myself paralyzed from the neck to the hips. My eyes and toes could be moved slightly. My body was numb. I could not tell whether I was breathing or whether the heart was beating.

Through my brain fog there materialized above me what appeared to be a two-headed face because my vision was out of focus. I then realized that my eyeballs were at different levels and that my head was encased in a helmet-type bandage. As a doctor I knew what this meant: somehow my skull had been split apart enough to shift the eye sockets; that would explain the lack of feeling and motion. But why was I alive? (pg. 209)

I found out later that my scalp, which had been lacerated from my eyelid to the back of my head, was miraculously healed. The 180 plus stitches lay unneeded. The jagged red lines were firmly closed, and there was color in my face! (pg 212)

Later, I woke to hear a cheerful and familiar voice. There stood my colleague, Dr. Lay, a female doctor skilled in cranial manipulation to align distortions in the head bones. "Let's get this head on straight!" she quipped as she reached for my head. *"Oh my God. I didn't know it was this bad,"* she exclaimed, noting the two halves out of line. *"They sewed the scalp over the skull without putting it back together! How do you function at all? Never saw the likes of this before. But here goes."* She gently held the crooked head and began molding it back toward normal. In an hour my eyes began to focus; the lop-sided jaw would now close; my ears were almost level; and the ugly ridge along the skull was disappearing as the sutures slid together. After a few more treatments the structure of the head was nearly restored, my functions were improving daily.

A few days later I was home and my blood count was normal despite having been "bled out" and no transfusions. My brain function was essentially normal aside from the residual dizziness from the damaged inner ear and my hair quickly grew out from the sutured scalp, thicker than before. Above all, I was experiencing a new companionship with God. (pgs 214-216)[9]

Pastor Yonggi Cho

Yonggi Cho is the pastor of Yoido Full Gospel Church (Assemblies of God) in Seoul, South Korea, which has the world's largest congregation with a membership of more than 850,000.

Pastor Cho was speaking at a meeting when he received a call from his wife "Come home, your son is dying." (This was his second son, Samuel, now a schoolboy. His mother had discovered to her surprise, through a dream about Hannah, that he had been conceived. She was told it was a boy and was to be Samuel—a most unusual name in Korea.) Samuel was one of eight schoolboys who had already died from eating deep-fried silkworms sold by a street vendor. The country farmer who brought the catch to town used packaging that was previously used for insecticide.

The boy's last message as he lay in his father's bed was "Tell Daddy to pray for me but I'm pretty sure I'm going to heaven tonight." Cho arrived home to find his wife frantic. He began to cry out "No Samuel! You cannot go away." Then, kicking off his shoes, he crawled to the middle of the bed beside the lifeless body and prayed, "Father, I will not let my boy go!" He found it hard to pray and his words sounded hollow. He did two things. He closed his eyes and focused on the healthy robust picture of the son he remembered Samuel to have been—a well-rounded boy, leader of the pack- a sportsman skilled in the traditional art of self-defense.

He also began to ask God's forgiveness for every wrong that came to mind—not in generalities, but exact sins… the times he had wronged his wife in word or deed, his ingratitude for his children, etc. This went on for an hour or two. When he opened his eyes again, Samuel, his son, still appeared lifeless—impossible to rouse or communicate with. He began to plead with God till past midnight. The focus of his imagination was not on the lifeless body beside him, but on the tall, vigorous and jovial Samuel he wanted to see again.

Then he got off the bed and, facing the boy, he thundered "Samuel!", clapping his hands in a loud jolting manner. "Samuel! In the name of Jesus Christ of Nazareth, rise up and walk!" The boy sprang to his feet, whilst Cho almost fell backward in fear. Samuel crumpled and fell halfway across the bed, vomiting. He gestured with his hand, "Say hello to Jesus, Papa." He repeated it, "Say hello to Jesus. He's right there." The boy pointed. His father bowed toward the place indicated and said softly, "Hello Jesus."

"Didn't you see us coming down the hallway? Didn't you see us, Papa? Jesus carried me in his arms. He was carrying me to a *beautiful* place—brighter than anything I've ever seen—the most beautiful music my ears have ever heard. I couldn't recognize the tune, but we kept getting closer and closer to it. Then Jesus said to me, 'We have to go back.' 'No', I said. 'Yes, we have to go back. Your father won't let you go.' And he was bringing me back to the bedroom. Didn't you see us coming down the hall? You were calling me and you commanded me to get up. That's when Jesus let go of me. There He is—Oh, He's not there. He must have gone back, I guess."[10]

David Hogan

In the small Southern Mexico village of Chiconamiel, an epidemic of black measles swept through in 1998 and quickly killed about forty people. Two of the victims were teenage girls, daughters of a widow who was a fairly new Christian. By the time the girls died, there was no one left in town healthy enough to help her carry the girls' bodies to the graveyard. So the poor woman had to drag both bodies there herself.

Because of the plague, there were only two young men strong enough to dig graves, so there was a line of 21 corpses waiting to be buried. The woman tenderly laid the bodies at the end of the line, and since it was hot, sprinkled a lot of white lime powder over the bodies as a disinfectant. Then set off walking down the mountain.

The next morning, after eight hours of walking, she reached the town where her Christian contacts lived. But since the men were in the middle of a heavy prayer and fasting meeting, she had to wait two hours more to see them. By that time, they didn't think they could climb back up the hill to Chiconamiel before nightfall, so they waited till the next morning.

When they finished the uphill trek, it was evening again, and the girls' bodies were only three or four away from being buried. The men gathered around the bodies in a circle, as the disciples did for Paul when he had been stoned and left for dead in Acts 14:19. They prayed in the authority of the Lord Jesus Christ, and they called the girls by name. Both of the dead girls sat up!

The young men then had a good laugh as they watched the girls trying to spit the lime powder out of their mouths. This is but one of the many highly varied occurrences in southern Mexico (plus the highlands of Guatemala) that have sprung from the work of Freedom Ministries staff. To date, they have seen over 300 come back from death. (They've stopped counting.) This is the world's major epicenter of resurrections.

Freedom Ministries was founded and is led by David Hogan, a boisterous but very cautious American who has been present at 22 of these events. He no longer rushes to the scene of a reported death when they send for him. Like Jesus with Lazarus, he often delays in order to complete previous ministry assignments God has given him. And when he does arrive, he preaches a sermon to the bystanders. Gospel first, resurrection afterward![11]

Ronny Sampson

Ronny Sampson is a retired businessman who was enjoying a quiet visit with his daughter in Johannesburg, South Africa, when loud screaming sent him running into the street. There he found a hysterical woman carrying the body of her daughter, which had just been found at the bottom of a swimming pool. Sampson commented later, *"Nobody knew how long she had been there, but she was completely blue, had no pulse, and had ceased breathing."*

While others called an ambulance, Simpson took the women and child into his daughter's house and started to pray. After twenty frustrating minutes of fruitless prayer, he finally became quite angry and started shouting loud commands at the *"spirit of death"* that held the girl.

That made the difference. Suddenly, the child turned over, regurgitated huge amounts of water, and started to scream. In fact, her screams, combined with those of her still distraught mother, helped the ambulance find the house quickly.

The paramedics pronounced the girl completely healthy, and examinations showed there was no brain damage. A Dutch television team came from Holland and made a docudrama of the event.[12]

Around the World

James Rutz shares the following:

Resurrections have been reported in the following 52 countries. And I'm not referring to "near death experiences" (NDEs), the common phantasm with a tunnel and a light at the end, where Buddhists meet Buddha, Catholics meet Mary, etc. I am talking about people who were stone dead for up to three days.

† Algeria Honduras Philippines

† Argentina India Romania

† Australia Indonesia Russia

† Bulgaria Iran Rwanda

† Burundi Kazakhstan Sierra Leone

† Cambodia Kenya Solomon Islands

† Canada Korea South Africa

† China Malawi Spain

† Congo Malaysia Sudan

† Cuba Mexico Sri Lanka

† England Mongolia Tanzania

† Ethiopia Mozambique Togo

† Fiji Myanmar (Burma) Uganda

† Finland New Zealand Ukraine

† Germany Nigeria United States

† Ghana Pakistan Vietnam

† Guatemala Panama

† Haiti Papua New Guinea

Why the sudden flood of resurrections? In part it is because Christians around the world are starting to realize, *we can do this!* In part it is because God is calling you and me to a new plane of existence. Are you ready to move up?[13]

Five Reasons for Resurrection

Here are five compelling reasons to raise the dead. They are common throughout the stories that we have read in this chapter.

1. **Evangelism:** What more powerful tool can be employed than the raising of the dead?

2. **Uncompleted destiny:** When Paul resurrected Eutychus after he fell out of the window, his destiny wasn't complete, he was just tired.

3. **Provision:** The widows who lost their sons to early death had need of someone to provide for them.

4. **Death is an enemy:** Anything that is an enemy of God should be resisted by His Church (see 1 Cor. 15:26).

5. **Jesus came to give us life, abundant life** (see John 10:10).

FINAL THOUGHTS

We have seen that raising the dead has always been part of Christian life since the times of the Old Testament. Even Abraham believed in the raising of the dead before one resurrection had ever occurred.

> *By faith Abraham, when God tested him, offered Isaac as a sacrifice. He who had received the promises was about to sacrifice his one and only son, even though God had said to him, "It is through Isaac that your offspring will be reckoned." Abraham reasoned that God could raise the dead, and figuratively speaking, he did receive Isaac back from death* (Hebrews 11:17-19).

Since Abraham could believe for the raising of the dead without any previous example to cite, then *"Why should it be thought incredible by you that God raises the dead?"* (Acts 26:8).

ACTIVATION

Create a resurrection preparedness letter. When the death of a loved one occurs, it is typical to go into shock. So before this situation presents itself, it is important to prepare those around you for what you want them to do in case of this emergency.

There are forms in the medical field that are signed when death is imminent; one of these forms is a *Do Not Resuscitate* form. This means that if an individual signs this form and then dies, medical professionals will not try to resuscitate the person. Consider writing the following letter as your *Do Supernaturally Resuscitate* form.

Sample Letter

To whom it may concern,

When I die, I am requesting that the following people are contacted immediately:

✝ Pastor John Smith

✝ Shelly Stevens

✝ John Brown

✝ Tim Berry

They are to be informed of my passing and requested to come and pray for my physical resurrection. I consider death to be an enemy, and I will not go quietly. I am asking for these individuals to come and stand by my body in prayer against the grip of death.

I request that these individuals would have the earliest possible access to pray over my body. They may bring their spouse or select other individuals of their choosing.

I ask that these individuals would fast for the duration of the time from when I die until they sense the release to cease praying for resurrection.

I ask that worship music would accompany my body as much as possible so as to set an atmosphere of hope and faith.

Sincerely,

Timothy Clark

(Now share this letter with your spouse or closest living relative, as well as with the individuals you have chosen to list.)

ACKNOWLEDGMENTS

To Douglas Johnson and Ruben Reyes. You have both loved me back to life and metaphorically raised me from the dead. I love you and am ever grateful for your friendship.

ENDNOTES

1. James Rutz, *Mega Shift, Igniting Spiritual Power* (Colorado Springs, CO: Empowerment Press, 2005), 3-4.

2. David Pychtes, *Spiritual Gifts in the Local Church* (Minneapolis, MN: Bethany House Publishers, 1985), 231-232.

3. Quoted from *The Life and Acts of St. Patrick*, translated from the original Latin of Jocelin, Cistercian monk of Furnes of the 12th century, by Edmund L. Swift, Esq., Dublin, 1809. Father Albert J. Hebert, *Raised from the Dead* (Rockford, IL: Tan Books and Publishers, 1986), 191-192.

4. Quoted from a Catholic source and while Protestants (myself included) would not agree on the doctrine of infant baptism, it is still a remarkable testimony showing that Joan of Arc moved in resurrection power. Father Albert J. Hebert, *Raised from the Dead*, 93.

5. *Ibid.*, 175, 178-179.

6. David Pychtes, *Spiritual Gifts in the Local Church*, 232-233.

7. Mel Tari, *Like a Mighty Wind* (Harrison, AR: Creation House, 1971), 76-78.

8. Dr. Richard E. Eby, *Caught up into Paradise* (Old Tappan, NJ: Spire Books, 1978), 200-202.

9. *Ibid.*, 202-216.

10. *Ibid.*, 236-237.

11. James Rutz, *Mega Shift, Igniting Spiritual Power*, 8

12. *Ibid.*, 12-13.

13. *Ibid.*, 29-30.

CHAPTER TEN

AUTHENTIC VERSUS COUNTERFEIT

...But as his anointing teaches you about all things...
that anointing is real, not counterfeit... (1 John 2:27).

A thought came to me as I walked the aisles of my local Christian book-store. I kept noticing row after row of *response books*. I have given them this label; I do not think they have a classification in the book world. A *response book* is a book written in reaction to the secular entertainment world. Typically these are written regarding the mega-bestsellers of the day or the blockbuster hit movies and most especially in reference to the flavor-of-the-month fads: a series about romantic vampires or a young British witch or a movie about the lost Gnostic gospels.

Once the secular world produces a success, Christian authors take to the task of writing a slew of reactionary books. Not that these books are inaccurate, but it seems to me that writing a book to tell Christians not to let their young children read books about witchcraft is insulting to the buyers' intelligence.

This approach puts the Church on the defensive in engaging the world. Our time is not best served by pointing out the darkness that surrounds us; we are to display our light. Considering that the best fiction writers of the 20th century, C.S. Lewis and J.R. Tolkien, were devout Christians, the Church has the power to shine brightly in the darkness.

We cannot spend precious time on the defensive against the onslaught of evil in the secular entertainment world. I would like to present a new strategy. Each time we see the kingdom of darkness highlighted through books, movies, and the like, we should ask, *What is this a counterfeit of in the Kingdom of Light?*

Throughout the Bible we see that everything satan does is a mere counterfeit of something from God's Kingdom. Apostle Paul calls these counterfeits, *masquerades.*

> *And no wonder, for Satan himself **masquerades** as an angel of light. It is not surprising, then, if his servants **masquerade** as servants of righteousness. Their end will be what their actions deserve* (2 Corinthians 11:14-15).

The devil is not a creative being; he operates his kingdom by masquerading as light. To masquerade means to have *an appearance that is a mere disguise.* In fact, if the nature of the devil were to be studied throughout the Bible, we would find that the only thing he can do is take something that God has created and distort it into something different and worse than it was originally meant to be. Jesus said that the nature of the devil's work is to steal, kill, and destroy (see John 10:10).

Counterfeits Reveal Authenticity

This brings us to the most important point of this chapter. *If there is a counterfeit, there is an authentic that we need to find and reclaim.* Every time we see a masquerade, we need to look closely to properly discern what is being counterfeited, because a counterfeit is evidence that an authentic exists.

Consider the example of counterfeit money. If there is counterfeit money, it proves that there is real, authentic money. Just because counterfeit money exists, we do not burn all our real money to avoid deception. The best response would be to get as many people as possible to use real money, so that when counterfeit money appears, it is recognizable by all.

The fact that there are people operating in counterfeit miracles proves that there are real miracles available to the Church. However, many Christians have tried to protect themselves from the counterfeits by avoiding miracles and staying far away from the supernatural. This is like burning all the money in your wallet because there are counterfeits in the world and deception is possible.

As Christians, when we see that satan has created a counterfeit, we commonly overreact to try to protect ourselves from contamination. One way that we overreact is by throwing out anything that looks like the counterfeit, including the real. Consider taking this as a personal challenge: *If you see a counterfeit, use it as a signpost that points to the authentic.* The idea that it is easier to throw out the gift from God altogether is a strong temptation, but a wrong choice. We have been commissioned not to throw out all things, but to *"Test everything. Hold on to the good"* (1 Thess. 5:21). Therefore, if we see a counterfeit, we must test it and find out what it counterfeits so we can reclaim the authentic.

THE SOURCE

The test to determine whether something is counterfeit or authentic is important, because the wrong testing method can lead us to the wrong conclusion. The Bible does not say, "Test all things and throw out all that are supernatural because those things passed away at the end of the apostolic age." Yet somehow this is where whole branches of the Church have settled down. Since that is a wrong test, these groups have created false doctrines that say God no longer uses the laying on of hands for healing, that speaking in tongues is not for today, that interacting with angels is strange, and that the dead are no longer raised to life in the modern age.

To test all counterfeits, both natural and spiritual, you must determine the source. A real Rembrandt painting is authentic because Rembrandt painted it. With counterfeit currency the question is, "Did this bill originate from the official government mint?" It does not matter that the counterfeit money or paintings look similar to the originals. The counterfeit was created with that precise intent: the best counterfeit looks as close to the original as possible, and it is difficult to tell the difference. The test of authenticity is always about origin. This is true of money, paintings, and the spirit realm.

Many Christians have been afraid to reclaim the authentic because they consider the power of the counterfeit to be overwhelmingly deceiving. The perception is that one could accidentally fall over the edge and suddenly be operating in the counterfeit without meaning to.

Personally, I have a lot more faith in the Lord's ability to keep me than in the devil's ability to steal me away. Jesus said that He has us in His hand and no one can snatch us out. *"I give them eternal life, and they shall never perish; no one can snatch them out of My hand"* (John 10:28). If we are asking the Lord to restore the authentic to us, why should we have so much fear of accidentally operating in the counterfeit? Jesus said:

> *Which of you fathers, if your son asks for a fish, will give him a snake instead? Or if he asks for an egg, will give him a scorpion? If you then, though you are evil, know how to give good gifts to your children, how much more will your Father in heaven give the Holy Spirit to those who ask Him* (Luke 11:11-13).

There is no need to fear the supernatural if we are Christians. God has us in His hand. If we are asking for the Holy Spirit to do something, we do not need to fear receiving a counterfeit. The way that God moves in power looks a lot like the New Age, and this has scared many Christians away from operating in the gifts of the Holy Spirit.

The truth is that the gifts of the Holy Spirit will look similar to the counterfeit. The New Age is a counterfeit, and the best counterfeits resemble what they are made to imitate. The counterfeit and the authentic will always look incredibly similar; the main test is the origin. We find this point powerfully illustrated in the case of Aaron and Moses having a confrontation with Pharaoh's magicians.

> *The LORD said to Moses and Aaron, "When Pharaoh says to you, 'Perform a miracle,' then say to Aaron, 'Take your staff and throw it down before Pharaoh,' and it will become a snake"* (Exodus 7:8-9).

At that time in history, magicians were well-known for turning their staffs into snakes. It is reasonable to wonder if Moses and Aaron were concerned how this miracle would make them look to their fellow Hebrews. This would be similar to God telling a local pastor to perform a miracle in the same way that the New Age or occult are known for performing miracles. If this scenario were to take place nowadays, I can imagine at least the three following reactions from Christians:

1. Some would accuse Moses and Aaron of operating in evil supernatural power, such as the religious leaders did with Jesus when He performed deliverance (see Luke 11:14-20).

2. Others would caution Moses and Aaron not to perform this miracle because it would look just like the sorcerers, and they could fall into deception.

3. Some would question whether God even talked to Moses, because surely God would not tell him to do something the magicians do.

> *So Moses and Aaron went to Pharaoh and did just as the LORD commanded. Aaron threw his staff down in front of Pharaoh and his officials and it became a snake. Pharaoh then summoned wise*

*men and sorcerers, and the Egyptian magicians also did the same
things by their secret arts: Each one threw down his staff and
it became a snake. **But Aaron's staff swallowed up their staffs***
(Exodus 7:10-12).

Moses won! When God is on our side, then we always defeat the counterfeits. The sorcerers performed an identical miracle; the only difference
was the source. Moses was sent from God. The sorcerers operated by "secret
(occult) arts." The only concern that the Church needs to entertain is to
make sure that we are walking in the power of God. We should not be afraid
that the counterfeit and the authentic look the same or what others will say
about us. If God is the Source, then the other powers will always be defeated.

We need to be much more concerned about reclaiming all of our stolen
goods from the enemy than about being afraid of the deception of counterfeits. We must be more aware of Paul's admonitions that we should *not
be ignorant of spiritual gifts* (1 Cor. 12:1) and that we should *strongly desire*
the spiritual gifts, rather than being fearful of them (see 1 Cor. 14:1). These
verses require more attention in the modern Church if we are going to
reclaim everything that the enemy has counterfeited.

THE TEST

One reason it has become increasingly difficult to discern the counterfeit from the authentic is that the New Age movement has been adopting
Christian language for the past several decades. They honor Jesus as a good
prophet, claim to interact with the "white light" of the Holy Spirit, and they
speak of God as their Father. This can confuse a Christian who does not
recognize the subtle, but important, differences between their language and
the truth of God's Word. I have stated that the main difference between a
counterfeit and the authentic is source, but we need to be even more specific
about how to discern between the two.

The test of what power source people are operating in can be boiled down
to the question, "Is Jesus the Lord of their lives?" According to Romans

10:9-10, people must acknowledge that Jesus was raised from the dead and that Jesus is the Lord of their lives. If people will not agree with these two things, then it is a fact that they are operating from a source other than the true Jesus of the Bible.

Spiritual practitioners who access and operate in the spirit without Jesus as the Lord of their lives are trespassers in the spirit realm. Jesus put it this way. *"I tell you the truth, the man who does not enter the sheep pen by the gate, but climbs in by some other way, is a thief and a robber"* (John 10:1). So to answer the common question, "Are psychics and New Agers operating in real power?" The answer is yes, but they have climbed in as trespassers. They have not accessed the spirit realm through Jesus.

God the Father is the Lord of Heaven and earth, and therefore, all realms are His (see Matt. 11:25). There is only one way to be in right relationship to the Father, and that is through His Son, Jesus (see John 14:6). It is Jesus who came to pay for our sins, bring us into correct relationship with the Father, and open the heavens and all the spirit realms to us (see John 1:15; Matt.16:19; Eph. 2:1-7; Col. 3:1-3). It is the authority of Jesus that protects us from the evil spiritual beings that dwell in the unseen realms.

Without receiving the death, resurrection, and forgiveness of Jesus, we are not in right relationship with the Father. Without right relationship, we are trespassing when we enter into spiritual experiences, and we can be easily deceived and destroyed. It is *dangerous* to operate in spiritual realms without being in right relationship with the Lord of Heaven and earth. We must go into the sheepfold through *the gate,* which is Jesus Christ.

There are many people who claim Jesus in their spiritual practices, but they have not actually submitted themselves to His lordship. I believe that these are the people Jesus was speaking of when He said:

> *Not everyone who says to Me, "Lord, Lord," will enter the king-*
> *dom of heaven, but only he who does the will of my Father who is*
> *in heaven. Many will say to Me on that day, "Lord, Lord, did we*
> *not prophesy in Your name, and in Your name drive out demons*

and perform many miracles?" Then I will tell them plainly, "I never knew you. Away from Me, you evildoers" (Matthew 7:21-23).

Unfortunately, many Christians have beat themselves up wondering if they are those to whom Jesus was referring in this passage. The truth is that this group is comprised of people who use Jesus' name, but have no personal, experiential, relationship with Him. This passage is referring to those in the New Age and other such movements that use Christian language, but have not submitted to Jesus as their Lord.

Resistance

As we have seen so far, there are many people who operate in the supernatural. Some operate safely under the lordship of Jesus Christ and some, such as Buddhists, Hindus, New Agers, and Occultists, operate dangerously as trespassers.

For the Normal Christian reclaiming the supernatural, the greatest resistance actually does not come from those who are walking in the counterfeit, but rather from a third group. Here are the three perspectives regarding the operation of the supernatural as I see it.

1. Those walking in the authentic.

2. Those walking in the counterfeit.

3. Those walking in neither and afraid of groups 1 and 2.

Interestingly, group 1 (Christians operating in the power of the Holy Spirit) typically receive the most opposition not from group 2 (false religionists operating out of evil power sources), but actually from group 3 (fellow Christians who believe false doctrines regarding the operation of supernatural power).

The counterfeit and the authentic look so similar that group 3 frequently declares that group 1 is walking in the counterfeit. This is similar to what the Pharisees said of Jesus.

> *One day Jesus cast out a demon from a man who couldn't speak, and when the demon was gone, the man began to speak. The crowds were amazed, but some of them said, "No wonder He can cast out demons. He gets his power from Satan, the prince of demons"* (Luke 11:14-15).

Like the Pharisees, the modern religious spirit does not understand that the existence of the false proves that there is an authentic. Instead of asking God for discernment to tell the difference, the Pharisees determined that if they look the same, then they are the same.

Considering that even Jesus Himself was accused of walking in dark, supernatural power, we should be prepared for the same accusation. As we reclaim our God-given gifts, there will always be those who accuse us of falling prey to the counterfeit. There is a theological failing that prevents them from seeing the truth. According to their own theology, all supernatural manifestations in this day and age are considered counterfeit. Everything supernatural is declared to be a lying sign and wonder.

By believing foolish doctrines such as cessationism (the false doctrine that miracles stopped after the supposed "age of the apostles"), much of Average Christianity has abandoned the authentic powers of God. I say this tongue-in-cheek of course, but according to some Christians, only satan's people are allowed to operate in the supernatural!

There is a crafty strategy that is often employed by the religious. For example, the religious will compare a certain branch of the Church with the world, and by drawing parallels, they instill fear and division in the Body of Christ. I have heard it said, "Since the false religion of Mormonism believes in speaking in tongues, then it must be of the devil; therefore, when Charismatics are speaking in tongues, they must be in collusion with the devil."

Being a Normal Christian is not for the faint of heart. There will always be those who resist the Holy Spirit. But what may surprise you (as you become Normal) is that the strongest resistance does not come from the sinner, but from the fellow saint. When you become Normal, you upset the status quo, and you force the Average Christian to begin a painful self-evaluation.

One of the main accusations from the quagmire of Average Christianity is that the authentic looks too much like the counterfeit. Considering that the purpose of a counterfeit is to imitate, this accusation is absurd, and this convoluted logic shows their fear of the darkness. We were not meant to fear evil, but to overcome it with good.

As we have discussed, the religious Christian often resists the Holy Spirit, whereas the nonbeliever is more likely to be intrigued and possibly converted. For example, consider how Simon the Sorcerer responded to Peter (see Acts 8). Simon was willing to pay money to have the power of the Holy Spirit!

Those who are living their lives in darkness are powerfully drawn toward the bright light of Truth. Conversion is the typical response when the world encounters Normal Christians walking in the authentic.

COUNTERFEITS TO RECLAIM

With all this talk about counterfeit and authentic, by now you may be scratching your head hoping for examples. The best examples I have found are in the New Age Movement. They have been trafficking in the Church's stolen goods for a long time. Here are some examples of what has been counterfeited. These actually belong to the Church, but they have been stolen and cleverly repackaged.

AURA

The name given to the enveloping energy that surrounds and radiates from natural objects, including human beings, animals, and plants. The colors and forms of each aura are believed to be characteristic of the person, animal, or thing it surrounds and to fluctuate and shift according to mood and state of health.

What is referred to as the *aura* is the same concept as the human spirit, except that the term *aura* also implies the idea that an individual can carry a certain power in them. This is a strongly biblical concept. The Bible teaches that a believer's spirit is one with the Holy Spirit. *"He who is joined to the Lord is one spirit with Him"* (1 Cor. 6:17 NKJV).

This means that the human spirit is radiating the power of the Holy Spirit through us wherever we go. Healing is a very common manifestation in Scripture of how this power affects others. For example, the apostle Peter was known for radiating so much of the Spirit of God in his human spirit that people lined the streets in hopes that his shadow would touch and perhaps heal them.

> *As a result, people brought the sick into the streets and laid them on beds and mats so that at least Peter's shadow might fall on some of them as he passed by. Crowds gathered also from the towns around Jerusalem, bringing their sick and those tormented by evil spirits, and all of them were healed* (Acts 5:15-16).

Of course, Jesus Himself had the Holy Spirit flowing out of His Spirit and bringing healing to people. On one occasion when Jesus was close to being physically crushed by a crowd, a woman was suddenly healed when she reached out and touched Him in faith. Of all the people who were touching Jesus at that moment, only one pulled spiritual substance out of Him. *"At once Jesus realized that power had gone out from Him. He turned around in the crowd and asked, 'Who touched My clothes?'"* (Mark 5:30). Spiritual substance can be carried in the spirit of a person and even released to others.

Clairvoyance

The word *clairvoyance* comes from the French, meaning "clear seeing" and refers to the power to see an event or an image in the past, present, or future. This type of sight does not happen with your physical eyes, but with your inner eyes (second sight, sixth sense).

> Just as we have five senses which provide us with information about the physical world, we also have senses in touch with the spiritual world. The spiritual senses are just as important as the physical senses. Unfortunately, most of us have not developed our spiritual senses.
>
> Many Christians do not even believe they have any spiritual senses. I like to ask them, "Has the devil ever tempted you?" Of course, they answer yes. Then I like to say, "Well, how did you hear the devil? You could not hear him if you did not have spiritual ears." It is sad, but many people have more faith that the devil talks to us than that God talks to us. In reality, the Bible makes it clear that we all have spiritual eyes and ears.
>
> When Elisha prayed for his servant, he did not pray for God to give him eyes, but he prayed that God would open up his eyes (see 2 Kings 6:17). In Ephesians 1:18, Paul did not pray for the saints to receive eyes, but for God to open the eyes of their hearts. We already have spiritual eyes and ears. What we need is to have them opened. We need to become sensitive."[1]

CLAIRAUDIENCE

The word *clairaudience* comes from the French and means "clear hearing"; it is the ability to receive impressions of sounds, music, and voices that are not audible to normal hearing.

There are times when God will speak to an individual in a voice that is audible to the human ear, but that is not the same as clairaudience. Clairaudience refers to hearing in the spirit realm with the spiritual ear. In John 4:24, the Bible tells us *"God is spirit";* therefore, He will talk to us spiritually in our spiritual ears. Many people expect that if God, the Creator of Heaven and earth, is going to speak, then it would be earth-shaking and deeply profound. Yet when we read the Bible, we find that God more often seems to speak very subtly and softly, such as when He spoke to Elijah the prophet.

> *Then He said, "Go out, and stand on the mountain before the LORD." And behold, the LORD passed by, and a great and strong wind tore into the mountains and broke the rocks in pieces before the LORD, but the LORD was not in the wind; and after the wind an earthquake, but the LORD was not in the earthquake; and after the earthquake a fire, but the LORD was not in the fire; and after the fire **a still small voice.** So it was, when Elijah heard it, that he wrapped his face in his mantle and went out and stood in the entrance of the cave. Suddenly a voice came to him, and said, **"What are you doing here, Elijah?"** (1 Kings 19:11-13)*

We can notice two things from this passage about how we hear God in the spirit. Most often He speaks to us softly in a small voice. Even though we might think that God would speak through a strong wind, an earthquake, or a fire, He will surprise us by talking in a still, small voice.

The second insight is that God asks a question for which He already has the answer. Many people assume that God is like a guru sitting on top of a mountain with a long white beard, who only says deeply profound and mysterious things. This is not the God of the Bible. The God of the Bible is our Father who loves us with all of His heart. He walked and talked daily in the Garden with Adam and Eve. The apostle John was able to lay his head on the chest of Jesus because of their friendship. God is very personal, and He desires to communicate with us personally, not as a mystic, but as a loving Father to a child.

In human communication, the two main senses we use most often for relating information are sound and sight. Communication in the natural is comprehended through listening as well as through body language and facial expressions. God also communicates through the other three senses (taste, touch, and smell), but most of the time He will speak through seeing and hearing. Because the spiritual senses of taste, smell, and touch are the least understood, the following examples show how, on occasion, God may speak to us through these senses.

CLAIRSENTIENCE

The word *clairsentience* comes from the French and means "clear feeling or sensing." It involves the ability to pick up information through the senses of smell, taste, or touch. Feeling what is around you is the most common way to receive extrasensory information.

Taste

> *And He said to me, "Son of man, eat what is before you, eat this scroll; then go and speak to the house of Israel." So I opened my mouth, and He gave me the scroll to eat. Then He said to me, "Son of man, eat this scroll I am giving you and fill your stomach with it." So I ate it, **and it tasted as sweet as honey in my mouth"** (Ezekiel 3:1-3).*

If we suddenly taste something sweet, sour, salty, etc., but the taste is not a result of anything we have physically eaten or drunk, we should ask the Lord if He is trying to speak to us. On occasion, in the Old Testament, God spoke to His prophets through experiences with spiritual taste.

Smell

But thanks be to God, who always leads us in triumphal procession in Christ and through us spreads everywhere the fragrance of the knowledge of Him (2 Corinthians 2:14).

In many of my meetings, I have smelled Heaven's fragrances. I have come to understand that when I smell this sweet perfume, I am actually experiencing the physical manifestation of God smiling. The Bible says, *"His cheeks are like beds of spice yielding perfume"* (Song of Sol. 5:13). My insight is that when He smiles, His cheeks release the beds of spice into the atmosphere.

Touch

*...As Jesus was on His way, **the crowds almost crushed Him.** And a woman was there who had been subject to bleeding for twelve years, but no one could heal her. She came up behind Him and touched the edge of His cloak, and immediately her bleeding stopped. **"Who touched Me?" Jesus asked.** When they all denied it, Peter said, "Master, the people are crowding and pressing against You." But Jesus said, **"Someone touched Me; I know that power has gone out from Me"*** (Luke 8:42-46).

This is a great example of the difference between physical touch and spiritual touch. According to this story, Jesus was almost physically crushed, but when someone reached out and drew healing power out from His Spirit, He declared that someone had touched Him, speaking spiritually of course.

MEDITATION

Meditation is a contemplative technique of focusing your concentration on a specific object or thought for self-improvement or spiritual growth. The false religions of the world—Hinduism, Buddhism, Islam, and the New Age, to name a few—teach that meditation is emptying the mind to have spiritual experiences. This is their understanding of meditation.

The Bible teaches us to meditate in a fundamentally different way—it directs us to fill our minds, not empty them. The Bible even tells us what to fill our minds with. In the Word, there are at least four categories on which we are to meditate.

1. Meditate on Good Things

Finally, brethren, whatever things are true, whatever things are noble, whatever things are just, whatever things are pure, whatever things are lovely, whatever things are of good report, if there is any virtue and if there is anything praiseworthy—meditate on these things (Philippians 4:8 NKJV).

2. Meditate on the Word of God

Do not let this Book of the Law depart from your mouth; meditate on it day and night, so that you may be careful to do everything written in it. Then you will be prosperous and successful (Joshua 1:8).

3. Meditate on Prophetic Words

Do not neglect the gift that is in you, which was given to you by prophecy with the laying on of the hands of the eldership. Meditate on these things; give yourself entirely to them, that your progress may be evident to all (1 Timothy 4:14-15 NKJV).

4. Meditate on the Works of God

And I said, "This is my anguish; but I will remember the years of the right hand of the Most High." I will remember the works of the LORD; surely I will remember your wonders of old. I will also meditate on all your work, and talk of Your deeds (Psalm 77:10-12 NKJV).

I remember the days of old; I meditate on all Your works; I muse on the work of Your hands (Psalm 143:5 NKJV).

POWER OBJECTS

Any object that is believed to be a source of supernatural or magical power and which then confers its power to those who possess it is called a power object, including talismans, amulets, fetishes, psychometry, charms, and crystals.

The Bible shows us that it is true that physical objects can contain spiritual power and can even transfer that power to others through touch. The first example is the apron of the apostle Paul.

God did extraordinary miracles through Paul, so that even handkerchiefs and aprons that had touched him were taken to the sick, and their illnesses were cured and the evil spirits left them (Acts 19:11-12).

It is obvious from this example that physical objects can carry power and anointing. The second example would be the bones of the prophet Elisha.

Elisha died and was buried. Now Moabite raiders used to enter the country every spring. Once while some Israelites were burying a man, suddenly they saw a band of raiders; so they threw the man's body into Elisha's tomb. When the body touched Elisha's bones, the man came to life and stood up on his feet (2 Kings 13:20-21).

Resurrection power was dwelling in the bones of Elisha. It is evident that God's power can reside in a physical object. A third example would be the garment that Jesus was wearing when the woman who had been bleeding for 12 years was instantly healed (see Luke 8:43-46).

SPIRIT GUIDE

A spirit guide is a discarnate entity, often perceived as the higher self or a spirit of the dead that serves as a communications bridge, guardian, or guide. In shamanism, the spirit guide is known as a totem animal; in spiritualism, it is known as the medium's control; in witchcraft, it is known as a familiar (totem spirit, familiar spirit).

All Christians have a Spirit Guide who travels with them. The term *spirit guide* is somewhat scary to most Christians, yet this is a concept alluded to by Jesus Himself.

> *I have much more to say to you, more than you can now bear. But when He, **the Spirit** of truth, comes, He **will guide you** into all truth. He will not speak on His own; He will speak only what He hears, and He will tell you what is yet to come* (John 16:12-13).

When New Agers refer to spirit guides, they are actually referring to the evil spirits with which they commune. We who are Christians have an infinitely superior "Spirit Guide"—the Comforter, the Encourager, the one and only Holy Spirit. He is the most gentle, kind, perfect, wise, loving Spirit, and He guides us into all truth. We have access to Him day and night.

TRANCES

This is a state between sleeping and waking when a person is half conscious and focusing exclusively on internal thoughts and visions and is unaware of the surroundings. In the Greek language, the word *trance* is translated as "a displacement of the mind."

There are several examples of trances being a Normal Christian experience in the Bible; most notable are the cases of Peter and Paul.

Peter

*About noon the following day as they were on their journey and approaching the city, Peter went up on the roof to pray. He became hungry and wanted something to eat, and while the meal was being prepared, he fell into a **trance**. He saw heaven opened and something like a large sheet being let down to earth by its four corners. It contained all kinds of four-footed animals, as well as reptiles of the earth and birds of the air* (Acts 10:9-12).

*I was in the city of Joppa praying, and in a **trance** I saw a vision. I saw something like a large sheet being let down from heaven by its four corners, and it came down to where I was* (Acts 11:5).

Paul

*When I returned to Jerusalem and was praying at the temple, I fell into a **trance** and saw the Lord speaking. "Quick!" he said to me. "Leave Jerusalem immediately, because they will not accept your testimony about me"* (Acts 22:17-18).

These examples are merely to whet your appetite. This is just a small sampling. I have found throughout Scripture at least 75 examples of things that the New Age has counterfeited. However, I did not have space to include them all in this book. These examples have been included to stretch you and get you thinking differently about some of the ways that you may have reacted when you saw the counterfeits. Now whenever you see a counterfeit, I hope you will ask yourself these questions, "What is that a counterfeit of? What is its source? How can I have the authentic?"

THE COMMISSION

Imagine that the Church had a warehouse full of 10,000 nuclear warheads and that among these warheads were 100 false, nonworking warheads. Rather than testing each one for the true and false, the Church gave all 10,000 warheads over to our enemy and said, "We just don't want to be deceived by false warheads; perhaps we will be safer by throwing out anything that looks like a warhead."

This is essentially what happens when we respond to counterfeits out of fear. If we have an attitude that says, "If anything supernatural or beyond my understanding happens, then it must be of the devil," then we have already been deceived. This perspective leaves us with no true discernment and leaves us powerless against the enemy.

Counterfeits should be used as signposts. Every time a counterfeit shows up, *take it as the Lord presenting you with an opportunity to reclaim the authentic from the darkness.* Take up the cause to reclaim the Church's stolen property.

In the Old Testament, it says that when a thief is caught he must repay double what he stole (see Exod. 22:3-17). There is a time coming when the Church will realize that we have been robbed of our supernatural goods and that we must confront the thief. When we catch the thief (satan), he will come face-to-face with the fact that he has launched the Church into double the spirituality and power that we had before he robbed us. Retribution day is coming. We just have to identify the counterfeits and reclaim our stuff.

The best way to spot a counterfeit is to become an expert of the authentic. When you see a counterfeit, don't shrink back in fear—let this cry rise in your heart, *"That is mine, and I want it back!"*

ACTIVATION

What counterfeits came to mind while reading this chapter? Think of three, if you can. Now using these as guideposts, determine what they could be counterfeits of. List these as well.

ACKNOWLEDGMENTS

To my friend Mr. Kasey Miles. I am so thankful that God rescued you from the counterfeit and brought you into the true light. It has been such an honor being part of your journey of walking in the light. I am so proud of you, and I will always stand with you. I love you, man.

To Jacqueline Frattare. Without your constant pushing and prodding, this book may have never been written. Thank you. Your inquisitiveness and energy have brought such joy into my life. You are a constant reminder of why I do what I do. Love you!

ENDNOTE

1. Harold Eberle, *Partnership Newsletter* (Ykima, WA: World Cast Ministries, May 2008).

EPILOGUE

W hile many authors write whole books on each of the following topics, I chose to write one book encompassing all of them. This indeed is a lofty goal, and I realize that in the confines of this book I cannot plumb the depths of each of these topics. I have given my most valiant effort to share with you what I believe is **Normal Christianity**. Here is one final review of what I hope you have taken away from this book.

Topic	Average Christianity	Normal Christianity
Revival	Spontaneous	Lifestyle
Love	Performance	Unconditional
Affection	Cold/Distant	Warm/Embracing
Identity	Slave	Bondservant/Friend
Conscience	Condemning	Cleansed
Prayer	Weak/Wimpy	Powerful/Authoritative
Women in Leadership	Male Chauvinism	Equality/Honoring
End Times	Negative/Fearful	Optimistic/Victorious
Raising the Dead	Death Accepted	Death is Enemy
Counterfeit	Fearful	Evidence of Authentic

About Jonathan Welton

A fifth generation believer, Jonathan Welton is propelled by a power-ful Christian heritage. Exhibiting extraordinary wisdom as a teacher, he helps individuals discover fresh experiences of Kingdom realities. Even those who have grown up in the Church are challenged afresh as they hear the unique perspective that Jonathan carries.

Jonathan has earned two Masters Degrees, one in Biblical Studies and the other in Practical Ministry, as well as the National Herald of Christ award. Jonathan is the best-selling author of *The School of the Seers: A Practical Guide on How to See into the Unseen.* He and his wife, Karen, live in Rochester, New York.

For More Information and Exclusive Resources
www.JonWelton.com

In the right hands, This Book will Change Lives!

Most of the people who need this message will not be looking for this book. To change their lives, you need to put a copy of this book in their hands.

> *But others (seeds) fell into good ground, and brought forth fruit, some a hundred-fold, some sixty-fold, some thirty-fold* (Matthew 13:8).

Our ministry is constantly seeking methods to find the good ground, the people who need this anointed message to change their lives. Will you help us reach these people?

> *Remember this—a farmer who plants only a few seeds will get a small crop. But the one who plants generously will get a generous crop* (2 Corinthians 9:6).

EXTEND THIS MINISTRY BY SOWING
3 BOOKS, 5 BOOKS, 10 BOOKS, OR MORE TODAY,
AND BECOME A LIFE CHANGER!

Thank you,

Don Nori Sr., Founder
Destiny Image
Since 1982

DESTINY IMAGE PUBLISHERS, INC.

*"Speaking to the Purposes of God for This Generation
and for the Generations to Come."*

VISIT OUR NEW SITE HOME AT
WWW.DESTINYIMAGE.COM

FREE SUBSCRIPTION TO DI NEWSLETTER

Receive free unpublished articles by top DI authors, exclusive

discounts, and free downloads from our best and newest books.

Visit www.destinyimage.com to subscribe.

Write to: Destiny Image
P.O. Box 310
Shippensburg, PA 17257-0310

Call: 1-800-722-6774

Email: orders@destinyimage.com

For a complete list of our titles or to place an order
online, visit www.destinyimage.com.